D1760975

DANGEROUS

Praise for the serie

It was only a matter of time before a clever publisher realized that there is an audience for whom *Exile on Main Street* or *Electric Ladyland* are as significant and worthy of study as *The Catcher in the Rye* or *Middlemarch* … The series … is freewheeling and eclectic, ranging from minute rock-geek analysis to idiosyncratic personal celebration—*The New York Times Book Review*

Ideal for the rock geek who thinks liner notes just aren't enough—*Rolling Stone*

One of the coolest publishing imprints on the planet—*Bookslut*

These are for the insane collectors out there who appreciate fantastic design, well-executed thinking, and things that make your house look cool. Each volume in this series takes a seminal album and breaks it down in startling minutiae. We love these. We are huge nerds—*Vice*

A brilliant series … each one a work of real love—*NME* (UK)

Passionate, obsessive, and smart—*Nylon*

Religious tracts for the rock 'n' roll faithful—*Boldtype*

[A] consistently excellent series—*Uncut* (UK)

We … aren't naive enough to think that we're your only source for reading about music (but if we had our way … watch out). For those of you who really like to know everything there is to know about an album, you'd do well to check out Bloomsbury's "33 1/3" series of books—*Pitchfork*

For reviews of individual titles in the series, please visit our blog at 333sound.com and our website at http://www.bloomsbury.com/musicandsoundstudies

Follow us on Twitter: @333books

Like us on Facebook: https://www.facebook.com/33.3books

For a complete list of books in this series, see the back of this book

For more information about the series, please visit our new blog:

www.333sound.com

Where you'll find:

– Author and artist interviews

– Author profiles

– News about the series

– How to submit a proposal to our open call

– Things we find amusing

Dangerous

Susan Fast

BLOOMSBURY ACADEMIC
NEW YORK · LONDON · OXFORD · NEW DELHI · SYDNEY

BLOOMSBURY ACADEMIC
Bloomsbury Publishing Inc
1385 Broadway, New York, NY 10018, USA
50 Bedford Square, London, WC1B 3DP, UK

BLOOMSBURY, BLOOMSBURY ACADEMIC and the Diana logo are trademarks
of Bloomsbury Publishing Plc

First published in 2014
Reprinted by Bloomsbury Academic 2014, 2020

Cover design: Eleanor Rose
Cover image © Vince Cavataio/Getty Images

Library of Congress Cataloging-in-Publication Data
Jackson's Dangerous/Susan Fast.
pages cm. -- (33 1/3)
Includes bibliographical references and index.
ISBN 978-1-62356-631-9 (pbk. : alk. paper) 1. Jackson, Michael,
1958-2009. Dangerous. I. Title.
ML420.J175F37 2014
782.42166092--dc23
2014004659

ISBN: PB: 978-1-6235-6631-9
ePDF: 978-1-6235-6102-4
eBook: 978-1-6235-6156-7

Series: 33⅓, volume 100

Typeset by Fakenham Prepress Solutions, Fakenham, Norfolk
NR21 8NN
Printed and bound in Great Britain

To find out more about our authors and books visit www.bloomsbury.com
and sign up for our newsletters.

Track Listing

1. "Jam" (5:38)
2. "Why You Wanna Trip On Me" (5:25)
3. "In the Closet" (6:32)
4. "She Drives Me Wild" (3:41)
5. "Remember the Time" (4:00)
6. "Can't Let Her Get Away" (5:00)
7. "Heal the World" (6:25)
8. "Black or White" (4:16)
9. "Who Is It" (6:34)
10. "Give In To Me" (5:29)
11. "Will You Be There" (7:39)
12. "Keep the Faith" (5:57)
13. "Gone Too Soon" (3:24)
14. "Dangerous" (7:00)

Contents

Acknowledgments

This has been, simultaneously, among the most difficult and most rewarding writing projects I've ever undertaken. Difficult because trying to counter dominant narratives about Jackson and approach his work with the sophistication it deserves often felt daunting, especially given how little writing there is that takes up his art, rather than the mad media spectacle of his life; fulfilling because I shared the latter part of this journey with Willa Stillwater, Joseph Vogel and Lisha McDuff, three people who are among the few to have written seriously about Jackson's work, who have an encyclopedic knowledge of it, and who read drafts of every chapter as I completed it, offering extremely helpful critique; thank you Willa, Joe and Lisha for being so generous and supportive of this project. I was fortunate to be able to offer a graduate seminar on Jackson as I was finishing this project and am thankful for the enthusiasm and sharp thinking of the students in that class and their empathetic readings of Jackson and his work: Lakyn Barton, Jeffery Caldwell, MaryAnn Jazvac, Tonya Lazdowski, Timmy Mo, Justin Raymond, Sydney Saville, Amy Verhaeghe, and Chenfan Wu. Thanks to Matt Link, Stan Hawkins, Craig Jennex and Liss Platt for their comments on various parts of the manuscript. Liss, an artist, my colleague and friend, offered her expertise in interpreting the album cover, as did another colleague, art historian Alison McQueen. My thanks to them both. I'm grateful to David Barker for thinking the project worthwhile enough to be part of this series and Ally Jane Grossan and Kaitlin Fontana for expertly shepherding it through the editing and publication process. Finally, my deep-felt thanks to Michael for creating such magnificent music; the book is for those who already know that, but especially for those who don't yet.

Introduction

Telling Stories about Michael Jackson

1991's Dangerous *announced the end of Jackson's innocence and the command of a complicated, conflicted sensibility.*
Armond White

Dangerous is Michael Jackson's coming of age album. I know this is a grand and seemingly absurd claim to make, since many think his best work was behind him by this time. Let me explain. The record offers Jackson on a threshold, finally inhabiting adulthood—isn't this what so many said was missing?—and doing so through an immersion in black music that would only continue to deepen in his later work. Yet he was unable to convince a skeptical public, at this point wholly indoctrinated by the media, that he was either capable of grown-up senti-ments—by which I mean deep political engagement, adult expressions of sexuality, spiritual reflection—or interested in his black heritage. This in itself lays bare an interesting story, about what can in the end be told, believed, tolerated, condoned, accepted and by whom; a story about what it's possible to see (and hear) and what gets distorted, as the philosopher Ludwig Wittgenstein put it, by the fact that we often can't move beyond mental pictures of things that "hold us captive."[1]

The portrait of adulthood that we get on this record finds Jackson struggling with some weighty stuff—politics, love, lust, seduction, betrayal, damnation, and perhaps above all else race—in ways heretofore unseen in his music. He gives us a darker vision of the world, one based more in realism than his characteristic theatricality. Maybe it's theatrical realism, but nonetheless, it has a different feel from previous offerings; he seems, at times, to be at a genuine emotional breaking point, at others to be indulging in irony. Even the bright moments are surrounded by uncertainty, anger, betrayal, or ambiguity and taken as a whole, the album leaves little doubt that pain eclipses hope; this is not shiny, happy pop music. Jackson had covered some of this territory before, to be sure: the brilliant angst-ridden "Billie Jean" is the prototype. But on *Dangerous* it's deeper and more sustained and it's not only about deception of the fleshly kind—although that's certainly there—but about *losing* oneself to desire, about the state of the world, systemic racism, loneliness, the search for redemption and community, and it's dark. Not "paranoid" as so many critics have called it (why doesn't he get to explore and return to themes he thought were particularly rich and provocative, as so many artists do, without being given this label?), but worried, gut-wrenched, horny, disappointed, suspicious, and knowing. In his review for *Rolling Stone*, Alan Light noted Jackson's new "assertive" sexuality and called his best work, here and elsewhere, that which "reveals a man, not a man-child," that his "finest song and dance is *always* sexually charged, tense, coiled," that "he is at his most gripping when he really is dangerous."[2] While many may not have believed Jackson as "bad," it's difficult to deny that he really was perceived as dangerous by this point—that is, in fact, my argument in this book. In his 2011 monograph on Jackson—one of a scant few works devoted to a serious exploration of the music, which is pretty crazy for an artist of this caliber—Joseph Vogel comments that several critics, like Light, seemed sympathetic to the new direction taken on *Dangerous*; after Jackson's death, Jon Dolan even made the perceptive comparison to Nirvana's *Nevermind*, which toppled *Dangerous* from the number one spot on the *Billboard* charts and ushered in the age of grunge: "Jackson's dread, depression and wounded-child sense of good and evil have more in common with Kurt Cobain than anyone took the time to notice."[3] Vogel fleshes this idea out in his essay written 20 years after the release of *Dangerous*:[4]

> Sonically, *Dangerous* shared little in common with the work of fellow pop stars like Madonna, Whitney Houston, and Mariah Carey. Its vision was much more ominous and expansive…. [C]ontrary to conventional wisdom, by the end of 1991, Nirvana was as much 'pop' as Michael Jackson—and Michael Jackson was as much 'alternative' as Nirvana…. If indeed it is considered a pop album, *Dangerous* redefined the parameters of pop.

Like *Nevermind*—or U2's *Achtung Baby* from the same year—*Dangerous* offers a brooding, vulnerable leap into the breach, with as much, if not more, technical sophistication and a much broader stylistic palette. In fact I'd say its generic confusion is partly what makes *Dangerous* a difficult record to grasp. It certainly isn't only lyrics that take Jackson down that road, but new ways of using his spectacular, agile voice, the dark, industrial grooves, a revived allegiance to the sounds of black music—past (soul and r&b) and present (hip hop)—his all-grown-up image and his dancing in the short films. Instead of producing another sleek crossover record full of hit singles, he offered up a table of gritty funk and gospel, punctuated by a dripping metal ballad, with one of the great, emotionally unbridled guitar players, Slash, in tow: no return to the crisp cheerfulness of Eddie Van Halen here. Only "Heal the World" and "Black or White" follow the time-tested Jackson crossover formula, with "Gone Too Soon" a brief nod to his love of Great American Songbook style; predictably, "Black or White" was his only number one *Billboard* Hot 100 single off the album—ironic given that the short film for this song, the first released, presented his strongest statement about race relations to date, was wholly misunderstood and condemned, and was the first real sign of his danger. There were fewer top ten hits on this record than he'd had since *Off the Wall*. Nor was his new direction blessed with the armful of Grammys he was by now used to carrying home. Still, it did sell over thirty million copies around the world. And musically, it did have a significant impact. For one thing, Nelson George suggests that Jackson's new tense, clipped vocal style on *Dangerous* ushered in a whole new approach to r&b singing in the 1990s and beyond,[5] and Vogel remarks that "[Jackson's] R&B-rap fusions set the blueprint for years to come,"[6] a new approach, then, to making one important kind of grown-up black music.

Significant as that may be, this album has been one of Jackson's least celebrated, lumped together in that regard with *HIStory*, *Blood on the Dance Floor* and *Invincible*, his last three records, perhaps some of the most substantive music ever to have been obliterated by personal scandal, professional missteps, and, as Armond White put it in his review of *HIStory*, "[m]edia complaints [that] come down to white, middle-class spokespeople saying 'Shut up and entertain us.'"[7] Vogel makes the important point that in these last albums, "Jackson played a less mainstream [role] … he was the superstar who now spoke from the margins, from the perspective of the wounded or the forgotten."[8] He started taking more risks in these records, became more brashly political, more interested in adult sexuality, worrying less, it seems, about his commercial standing.

There's starting to be some reassessment of these albums in the wake of his death, when it seems safer to like Jackson's music, but a lot of folks stopped thinking about Michael Jackson as being musically significant after *Bad*; heck, there are those who think Jackson's first solo record, *Off the Wall*, was his greatest and that it was all downhill after that. But most stop at *Thriller*. *The New Yorker*'s Bill Wyman recently wrote: "One of the cruelties of stardom is that you never know when you've reached your apogee. For Jackson, decline set in almost as soon as [*Thriller*] fell out of the No. 1 spot, in April, 1984."[9] Just so we're clear, that would mean tracks like "Man in the Mirror," are part of a "decline." OK, got it. And Nelson George wrote that *Thriller* "should be the central point of reference" in thinking through the meaning and significance of Jackson's legacy.[10] I respectfully disagree. Dave Marsh wrote a whole (and pretty cruel) book in 1985 based on the premise that Jackson's heyday had come and gone. Interestingly, given that Jackson made four more records after that point, Marsh never bothered to reassess; in fact he posted the final chapter of this book on his blog after Jackson's death, accompanied by the inexplicable comment "it holds up."[11]

Jackson also suffered under the hipster idea that commercially successful music can't have much of a message (some rock music gets mysteriously exempted from this) and if this is measured by degrees then Jackson's OTT commercial success makes him about the least likely candidate for radical politics. In 1987, the influential scholar of African-American culture, Cornel West, called Jackson "a nonoppositional instance of commodification in black skin that is becoming more and more like candy, more radical than McDonald's, but not by much;"[12] like many, he had kinder things to say after Jackson died.[13] These narratives in popular music are indicative of the extent to which people get invested in a particular idea of what counts as "authentic," "radical" or countercultural in popular music; his commercial success and his ability—and desire—to move among wholly incompatible musical genres gave him little credibility in these areas. In the case of Jackson, though, there are, of course, other complications. He made music that is incredibly accessible and so it's easy to stop at the surface, even though in most of his songs and short films there's an awful lot going on below; it takes some work to articulate what that is, even if you immediately feel the depth of the music and his dancing in your soul. But in addition, many people got increasingly disappointed with or frightened by who Jackson appeared to be and so could no longer find a space through which to grasp his art as art. My argument is that it is precisely when he enters artistic maturity, marked, I think, with the making of *Dangerous*, that his aberrance becomes intolerable and that a critical blindness towards his music takes hold. Michael as quirky crossover *wunderkind*, fabulous; inhabiting adulthood as the sexy guy he was, with those looks, his love of kids and kid-like things, his failure to partner up, making blacker-sounding music and talking seriously about race, sex, and spiritual life: good God. We were kidding, we don't want him to grow up. Please give us our little boy back.

Here's what happens after the release of *Dangerous*: first, he is admonished for his "violent" and sexually charged "panther dance" in the "Black or White" short film—the first single released off the album and, remember, televised nationally and internationally to a generally stunned audience of about five hundred million people. His sexuality, long a source of speculation (he felt obligated to issue a statement in 1984 declaring he was *not* gay), continued to be considered improbable. I mean, not only *hetero*sexually improbable, but improbable in general, despite his often sizzling self-presentation (fake, most critics concluded). He is criticized for appearing whiter than ever when in fact he begins, especially from this point forward, to radically challenge ideas about race *and* gender through his constant metamorphosis. He is deemed musically irrelevant in the wake of grunge and hip hop, without recognition that there might exist considerable congruity between these musical shapes and the ones he was laying down. And he is, finally, publically shamed with an allegation of child sexual molestation in 1993. What better metaphor could there be for society's rejection of him as an adult man, what better castrating gesture? *Dangerous* is the document that sets the wheels of his spectacular fall from grace into motion.

But let's try not to drift into this tragedy again, a move so easy to make when thinking about Jackson, and one that so many writers indulge to the detriment of us learning anything new about his music; let's stay focused on the moment before it happened, the moment that started to open the door to a new Michael Jackson, a new artistic vision, a moment of considerable promise. Let's figure out what was there that became so very scary to some. Cut loose for the first time in his professional life from *all* his fathers (Joseph, Berry, Quincy: how many fathers can one kid take?), acting as his own executive producer on the project, authoring or co-authoring all but two tracks and working with hip, young producers like New Jack Swing's Teddy Riley, the album can be viewed as the culmination of his long struggle for artistic independence and control, for liberation from the guiding hand of paternal influence (I'm well aware that there are many who think that his departure from Jones was the beginning of the end of his artistic brilliance; I disagree). Gone, at least from public view, are the chimp, crazy publicity stunts like napping in the hyperbaric chamber and videos that pair him dancing with claymation rabbits or ghouls—no slight to those wonderfully inventive and playful images intended. They are replaced by him stepping out with Madonna, a steaming video with

Naomi Campbell, a passionate on-screen kiss with Iman, a photo shoot with Herb Ritts in which, according to one reporter (and perhaps millions of fans) "he never looked sexier."[14] They are replaced by the stunningly cathartic and unsettling "panther dance" of "Black or White," a new charitable foundation, and a revealing interview with Oprah Winfrey, not the hippest choice, perhaps, but significant that Jackson chose, after his long silence, to speak to a black TV personality—he was always most honest and forthcoming to the black press, too. These public expressions of maturation found voice in the music as well, a superb collection of edgy songs (yes, I'd put "Heal the World" in that category for reasons incomprehensible to most right now, but read on). After his death *Guardian* critic Ben Beaumont-Thomas raved that *Dangerous* revealed Jackson "at the peak of his powers, with his widest ever emotional range," that he is, on this album "revelatory," that in short the album is Jackson's "finest hour."[15] Agreed.

*   *   *

After a long hiatus, I came back to *Dangerous* through an odd coincidence in 2009, a few months before MJ died. Maybe it was a foreshadowing of our collective return to his legacy as an artist. The last time I could remember thinking about his *music* before that, as opposed to sensational stories about his "tragic" life, was in the mid-1990s when *HIStory* came out and I was reminded how much I loved the incisive funkiness of tracks like "Wanna Be Starting Something." While his tunes lived on my iPod, I didn't dial them up very often. Then, in March 2009, *American Idol* aired Michael Jackson week, undoubtedly a cross-marketing strategy intended to promote his upcoming *This is It* concerts. The performances were categorically awful; I would realize after suffering through countless tributes in the wake of his death that it is all but impossible for other artists to sing his songs. They work because of the life he breathed into them, because of his intensity, his exquisite vocal colors, his phrasing, his rhythmic intricacy and precision. None of this seems to be replicable in another singing body and trying to do it only points right back to Jackson's musical genius, his singularity as an artist. The only way to cover a Michael Jackson song is to blow it apart, turn it inside out, like Chris Cornell did with "Billie Jean." Even Adam Lambert with his vocal histrionics couldn't keep "Black or White" from sounding trite. The only performance remotely believable that night was Alison Iraheta's rendition of "Give In To Me." It awoke in me the memory of that ballad and Jackson's artistic forays into the world of adult pain. My brain was so used to associating him with "Beat It" and "Thriller" that I had forgotten the point in his work where he crossed, musically, from adorable into an emotional mess. Since I like my music bloody, this warranted a serious return to the source from whence this little gem sprang. I became obsessed; I nearly drowned in Jackson's music for months and months, lost not only in tracks on this exquisite record and the short films that went with it, but every other he made. When he died in the midst of my rediscovering his work I was perhaps more devastated than I would have otherwise been. What to do except write about this incredible artist, on whose art so little ink had been spilled, even if I'm not sure I'm always up to the task, especially as a white Canadian outsider to this music that is so much about racial politics in the U.S. I've tried to be sensitive to this in the pages that follow, to be aware of what I can and cannot know.

My trip back to *Dangerous* reminded me what a baroque—and noisy—album it is, from the ornate cover art by pop surrealist painter Mark Ryden, to its length (fourteen tracks, most of them five, six, even seven minutes long, stretching the capacity of the still relatively new CD format to its limits) and stylistic breadth, to Jackson's emotional and musical excess: an excerpt of the chorale finale to Beethoven's Ninth Symphony—really? The full-on Andraé Crouch choir in back-to-back songs? All the banging and clanking and breaking. Far removed from the gleaming *Off the Wall*, the concise brilliance of *Thriller*, and the clean, theatrical synth-pop of *Bad*, *Dangerous* is messy, industrial, excessive on every level. Like *HIStory* and *Invincible*, it doesn't want to stop: the songs are long, there are so many of them, listening leaves Jackson's guts all over the speakers, yours all over the room. Not that I'm particularly interested in taming any of this wondrous music, but it all makes more sense if it's thought of as a concept album. Alan Light criticizes the running order, commenting that "the sequencing of *Dangerous* often clusters similar songs in bunches when a more varied presentation would have been stronger,"[16] but the "clusters" give us a compelling narrative arc and delineate a number of themes Jackson wants to explore. The chapters in this book follow that arc, moving dialectically between song and the social. Chapter One, *Noise*, looks at the first two tracks, "Jam" and "Why You

Wanna Trip on Me," in which Jackson takes a wide-lens view of the fragmented and harsh state of the world. Chapter Two, *Desire*, takes up the next four songs about sex and romance, giving me an opportunity to reflect on Jackson's intricate play with gender and sexuality at this point in his career. The album takes an abrupt turn on "Heal the World" and "Black or White," two songs I discuss in Chapter Three under the heading of *Utopia*. There's some dystopia there too; underneath the pretty surface, these songs deal with issues of systemic racism. They also, however, introduce the voices of children, one of the most radical moves, I argue, that Jackson makes on this record. The songs from "Who Is It" through "Keep the Faith" form the spiritual center of the album; Jackson's downward spiral into loneliness, feelings of betrayal and his search for redemption in these songs are the subject of Chapter Four, which I've called *Soul*. The album comes full circle with the last and title track "Dangerous," almost ending where it began, and I talk about this return in the brief *Coda*.

Six Teddy Riley-produced songs open the album, assaulting the listener with their hard, angular grooves and noisy intros and endings. What has always fascinated me about this initial musical gesture on the album—one that takes up fully *half* of the whole record, offering the most stylistically congruent block of songs—is how black it sounds. The grooves are harder-hitting than the New Jack Swing Riley had previously created. Next to Bobby Brown's "My Prerogative," or sister Janet Jackson's "Miss You Much," tracks like "Jam" and "She Drives Me Wild" sound as though they belong to a distantly related musical universe. This no doubt stems from

Jackson's love of crisp, staccato, complex, knock-you-down rhythms, which have more in common with his idol James Brown than, well, Wreckx-N-Effect. Jackson makes heavy distortion a principle in his singing on these tracks; he shapes it in many different ways, but the fact is that this voice, equally capable of some of the most pristine, angelic timbres in the history of popular music, sometimes sounds as though it's going to disappear in the rasp. He's drawing on the long history of vocal distortion as a sound ideal in black music, from the blues, to r&b, to soul and funk: it's a retro soul sound in the early 1990s. He updates with the inclusion of multiple elements from hip hop. He demonstrated his virtuosity as a beat boxer in his 1993 interview with Oprah, when he spontaneously recreated the multi-layered groove to "Who Is It," revealing a hip side of his musical personality that perhaps many didn't know existed; astonishing how he could just *produce* that groove without a moment's hesitation. The kind of immersion in black music at the beginning of *Dangerous*, as well as later on, when he turns to gospel, speaks loudly about where he wanted to locate his new, independent musical self. Not that he hadn't always kept black music near the surface, no matter how "crossover" he was. And he'd continue in this direction with *HIStory* and *Invincible*, in fact working with cutting-edge black r&b producers and singers right up to his death. It offers an interesting counterpoint to the even lighter skin tone that emerged with the release of this album; those who thought he was turning his back on black culture might have listened more closely.

Given Jackson's ability to inhabit different musical genres and styles, it's unsurprising that he didn't stick with New Jack Swing throughout *Dangerous*. This would have been too stultifying, too predictable. But the song with which Jackson chooses to break the flow is jarringly dissimilar, its sweetness next to what we've just encountered almost sickening. "Heal the World" appears at the very center of the album in an attempt, I'd argue, to make it the principal message. Through it, Jackson tries (unsuccessfully, I think) to wash away the considerable world-weariness and relationship anxieties advanced at the beginning of the album, bringing him back to the (literal) voices and emotions of children, and it beautifully sets up "Black or White," Jackson's complex and contradictory statement on race. This vision of healing and unity is all but shredded by the three ballads that follow, another "cluster" of songs that could only have been offered one after another to build and sustain a kind of emotional apocalypse. I find it difficult to listen to all three in a row—it's heartbreaking, gut-wrenching. "Who Is It" and "Give In To Me" are the album's most devastating songs of betrayal and wounded love, two sides of the same coin, one offered in the language of soul, the other metal. I'm not convinced that these songs are about romantic love, at least not entirely. Together with "Will You Be There," this trilogy has more to do with spirit than with flesh. "Keep the Faith" attempts to pull us back from the brink, but with moderate success; it offers only a moment of relief, an inadequate antidote for our gutted emotions. The tender ballad "Gone Too Soon" devolves into the hardest, most industrial groove on the record, the title track "Dangerous," which brings Jackson back to one of his favorite subjects: the *femme fatale*. Musically, the record has come full circle, back to another funky Teddy Riley track, but emotionally our protagonist has moved through his pain to a hardened place that views woman as suspect and threatening, even if he seems pretty ready to lose himself in the seduction.

*　　*　　*

The work on this record, and elsewhere, is beautiful, clever, intertextually rich, emotionally exhilarating one moment, draining the next. The music, lyrics, dancing and the various ways that Jackson presented himself to his public at this point in his career are impossibly ambiguous—one of the reasons I've felt so compelled to write about this work and one of the primary reasons, I'm convinced, that he was considered dangerous: a huge part of his politics is not only that he transgressed social norms, but that his transgressions cannot be easily read. We celebrate all kinds of ("avant-garde") artists for taking some of the same risks, but not Jackson. How much of the D.A.'s enthusiasm for bringing Jackson down in 1993 rested upon a fear—not only his, but society's—of an adult *black* man who looked, moved, behaved and emoted like this in the glare of mainstream culture? Who had "funny" ideas about kinship that included kids, Hollywood divas, and animals. As Michael Awkward wrote shortly after *Dangerous* appeared, "The best Afro-American man imaginable to racist white men and women was a dead, castrated, and therefore, according to androcentric notions, feminized man."[17] That's a lot to unpack.

That all the richness of Jackson's work has been largely ignored for the sake of sensationalist accounts of his differently lived life is deeply disturbing. That the response to his difference undid him is painful to contemplate. That race, as well as claustrophobic ideas about gender probably played a significant part in that undoing is infuriating. Serious consideration of his art has taken a back seat to this kind of bigotry for much too long. So here, in these pages, I'm going to tell different stories about Michael Jackson, which I hope will help change, or at least modify, in some small way, the mental picture we have of him. They're stories that begin to put his later, increasingly political work front and center, hopefully allowing Jackson's mature artistic vision to emerge from the shadows, his adult self to be acknowledged and perhaps even embraced.

Noise

Noise accompanies every manifestation of our [modern] life. Noise is familiar to us. Noise has the power to bring us back to life. Luigi Russolo

Bring the Noise. Public Enemy

Press play on your copy of *Dangerous* and you enter Michael Jackson's decade of noisy music-making. The record begins with the sound of breaking glass, a sound heard again on a number of its tracks. His next album, *HIStory*, opens with what could pass for a futuristic engine misfiring as it starts up, followed by an explosion and Jackson's muffled shriek. *Invincible*, likewise, with ominous low rumblings and a series of electronic bombs dropping. Although we're swept right into the wicked groove of "Blood on the Dance Floor" without noisy preamble, the next track on that EP, "Morphine," is introduced by start-stop buzzings, bangings, and electronic tappings from which the funky, hard, industrial groove appears (it's almost always that kind of groove that emerges from these noises—hard from hardness, noisy from noise). These records are birthed out of violent noise: breaking, exploding, screaming, reminiscent of *Dark Side of the Moon* or *It Takes a Nation of Millions to Hold Us Back* and maybe both were influences. The music comes *through* something to get to our ears, something traumatic. On *Dangerous* many of the songs are birthed from noise, some of it less violent, some not—car engine and honking horn on "She Drives me Wild;" what I've always heard as the threat of an approaching train on "Dangerous" (could also be factory sounds, but why are they coming closer?); the slamming door and breaking glass on "In the Closet." And songs culminate in noise: the concluding thunder of "Jam" and "Why You Wanna Trip on Me." "Tripping" begins with a wailing guitar solo that has, musically, nothing to do with what follows: the use of noise to create disjuncture, disorientation. Yelling and banging on doors in "Black or White," carried out over music that's deemed "too loud;" resistance to parental intervention comes in the form of a wailing rock guitar riff (perhaps this is the moment at which we make sense of the opening to "Why You Wanna Trip on Me?"): "Eat this," says the child.

Maybe in the context of a Michael Jackson record these sounds can be understood as the sonic equivalent of massive spectacle: if you know Jackson's—or The Jacksons'—live shows, you know that bigger and noisier were the order of the day and that this became increasingly pronounced on his later tours. While the *Bad* show had begun with Jackson and his dancers quietly gathering on the stage in darkness, *Dangerous* opened with him catapulting out of an underground elevator shaft amidst a shower of golden fireworks (perhaps a reference to the fire that rains down on him at the end of the "panther dance" in the "Black or White" short film. If we make this connection, those are angry, not celebratory sparks). The chorus of "Jam," the first song of the show, was punctuated by firework explosions on either side of the massive stage, to the left and right of Jackson, who cued their firing on the backbeat with outstretched arms and pointed fingers. At climactic moments in his shows and starting already with the short film for "Bad," Jackson would let loose a primal scream ("hooooooo") that ripped through the heart of the song's texture like Armageddon itself had been unleashed. This is to say nothing of Jackson himself as noisy spectacle, outfitted on the *Dangerous* Tour in a gold fencing shirt, his loosely curled hair now down below his shoulders and over his face (the jheri curl run amok), his sculpted and painted face bedazzling; no dancers flanking him, no other body required to create the noise, at least initially.

Spectacle, yes, reproduced, or produced as sound— thrilling, electrifying, exhilarating, but sometimes also threatening, angry, and ominous. The noise helps create music that is cinematic: the "non-musical" sounds, as things like breaking glass and banging doors in the context of a piece of music are often called, bring in the visual, because unlike "musical" sound, which tends towards the abstract, they often signify particular things, can be associated more easily with specific material objects or ideas. Jackson's music generally leaned towards the theatrical and cinematic, but with the exception of "Thriller," he didn't incorporate "non-musical" sounds until *Dangerous* and then they started shaping his records in pretty significant ways.

The noise can also be read as a sonic enhancement of the self: on some level, especially the dark, ominous explosions come to represent Jackson's penchant towards mythic self-representation, towards the grandiose. But this noisiness is narratively about more than a cheap thrill, about theater, or ego. "[T]he world is not for the beholding," wrote Jacques Attali. "It is for hearing. It is not legible, but audible."[1] The noise on Jackson's later records situates the listener in a particular kind of world, the contemporary urban world of upheaval, disruption, instability, of false starts (so many of the electronic sounds are like that—hesitating, incomplete thoughts). It puts modern technologies—cars, trains, synthesizers … bombs—front and center in the sonic landscape. In some cases this noisiness is linked to rage—eventually his own, at the press, at racist cops and prosecutors, at the greedy parents of children—but on *Dangerous* it's about other things. The breaking glass sound with which the album opens reappears and comes to have particular meanings in the context of the short films for "Black or White," "Jam" and "In the Closet." In the "Black or White" short film, glass breaks when the frame of a poster enclosing Jackson's image is smashed as it falls to the ground after the father, angry with his son's loud music, slams the door behind which it hangs. This seems more about symbolically releasing Jackson and the power of his (or rock) music than it does about destroying him. Touché Michael. Perhaps more crucially, glass breaks again and again during Jackson's "panther dance" at the end of that short film, when he unleashes his profound rage against structural racism.[2] In the short film for "Jam," a ball—actually a globe—bursts out of the window of a dilapidated building, breaking the glass. It is, soon thereafter, kicked by the foot of a child and it reappears at the end of the film, picked up and bounced by that child like a basketball (which, in the hands of Michael Jordan, it has turned into throughout the film: look, here's what good things can be done with the world in the hands of a virtuoso). The globe reappears at the end of the short film for "Heal the World," held between the hands of a child and again in "Black or White," as a perch for two babies, one black, one white. And it appears yet again in the short film for "Will You Be There," passed from the hands of a child to those of an angel: maybe for safe-keeping, maybe because humans can't seem to manage it themselves, maybe to impress upon us that there is no separation between heaven and earth. The significance of the globe/world to *Dangerous* is hinted at in Mark Ryden's cover art for the album, where it occupies the center of the painting. So a fundamental idea, carried out across the album as well as most of the short films, is born, if not immediately in pictures, then in sound: something is breaking, is broken. Through the lyrics to "Jam" and "Why You Wanna Trip on Me" and later through the images in the short film, we come to understand that this breakage is a response to a world in crisis. Through pictures and later, on "Heal the World," through the sound of their voices, it becomes clear that children might be the ones to fix the world. Before you roll your eyes and call this vision hopelessly naïve, let me say that this is not where the narrative of this record ends up. It's a pretty idea that doesn't work out.

*   *   *

Noise has been a key idea in many musics of resistance in the West. Sonically, it was the loudness of r&b and rock 'n' roll and that noisy, persistent backbeat that caused hysteria in 1950's white culture. Dick Hebdige wrote about punk that it disrupted the dominant culture by turning everyday objects into visual noise (safety pins as jewelry, garbage bags as clothing), to say nothing of the sound of the music: brash, unpolished, accompanied by screeching vocals.[3] Long before any of that, Luigi Russolo and his Italian Futurist friends thought, at the turn of the twentieth century, that the noise of the modern, industrial cityscape would save music from mediocrity, conservatism, and listeners from dire boredom.[4] The politics in all these cases are different, of course, and need to be examined carefully within their specific contexts, but since there is a long and strong tradition in Western culture, especially white culture, that "music" is meant to be sound that is tamed through technical apparatuses such as form and tonality and aesthetic ideals of conventional beauty, bringing the noise means disruption of the status quo on some level and for some reason.

Probably the most politically important kind of noisy music in recent memory has been hip hop, where especially in the early days, noise was a guiding principle, a means through which, as Robert Walser notes, "to express dissent and critique, and to articulate the identity of a community that is defined as, or that defines itself as, noise."[5] In her path-breaking book on rap music—called, significantly, *Black Noise*—Tricia Rose talks about the politics of hip hop's noisy and disruptive soundscape, quoting a middle-aged white male colleague: "they ride down the street at 2 a.m. with it blasting from the car speakers and wake up my wife and kids. What's the point of that?"[6] The point, sir, is to unsettle the rhythms of your normative, privileged life, to wake you up (literally) to the condition of those less privileged. This comment reminds Rose of a time when "slaves were prohibited from playing African drums because, as a vehicle for coded communication, they inspired fear in slaveowners."[7] In this context, records like Public Enemy's *It Takes a Nation*, or N.W.A.'s *Straight Outta Compton* represent a kind of peak in the principle of using noise as a signifier for dissent and critique, creating some of the fattest, loudest beats, layers upon layers of samples including "non-musical" sounds like speaking, sirens, and machine gun fire, white noise hiss, and dissonant interjections on the backbeat, "in search of," Robert Walser writes, the "conflicted urban soundscape, where sirens and drills punctuate the polytextured layers of modernity."[8]

Although Jackson loved to experiment with sound and had always done so, I don't think it's a coincidence that his records get noisier in the wake of late 1980's hip hop.[9] I'd go as far as to say that the incorporation of noise is as big a part of his embrace of this music as the sampling, scratching, beatboxing, and guest MCs we first hear on *Dangerous*. Well, we can hardly say that beatboxing makes its first appearance on this record: Jackson had been doing it for years before that, using it as a means through which to lay down initial grooves for many of his songs—listen to the demo for "Beat It" released on the *This Is It* soundtrack. But with his more profound embrace of hip hop's noisy soundscape, he clearly also incorporated the resistive politics of that music, in his own way, with his own message. He did not "[fall] out of step with the world of pop music,"[10] as some critics assume he did; he adapted the sonic and political landscape of contemporary urban music in a way that allowed him to stay true to who he was as an artist—a technically-polished singer-songwriter-dancer, who was not a rebellious teenager, but a man in his early thirties. He had a generation on his hip hop and alt rock contemporaries, whose more blunt and angry expressions of dissatisfaction with the world were not only youthful, but born out of a profoundly different approach to music-making, a different kind of masculinity, and a different worldview. Willa Stillwater makes an important point about what seems like Jackson's late and perhaps somewhat tentative embrace of hip hop: by the time the radical politics of this music began breaking into the mainstream, Michael Jackson *was* the mainstream; his decision not to incorporate hip hop into his music "during its most crucial period of growth," was a way of supporting the movement by refusing to co-opt it, an appropriation by "the establishment" that would have served to undermine it.[11] In the lyrics to "Jam," Jackson references the baby boom, of which he is a part, coming of age and "working it out." In effect, he suggests that his generation bears responsibility for the state of the world and for posing solutions. Perhaps he felt that it was time to step it up.

Jackson's music is all about precision, skill, polish, subtlety, marks of someone who'd been at it for a while, someone whose aesthetic was, in a way, modernist in its attention to structural detail and unity. Nelson George has commented that, "Jackson is one of the few artists who actually straddles the soul and post-soul worlds.

While his concepts of showmanship date back to the chitlin' circuit, Jackson is brilliant at adapting new styles … to his needs. Straddling requires remarkable balance and the ability to adjust."[12] The politics expressed on *Dangerous* are not as direct as those in hip hop; you have to dig deep for some of them. But you can't say that this record simply appropriates, stylistically, without musical innovation or without having political substance. Toying with styles, conventions, with traditions of all kind, which he had absolutely mastered by the time of *Dangerous*, was often precisely where the source of his politics lay.

*   *   *

There is a way in which Jackson's stylized, blunt, clichéd, but raw form of moralizing in his more overtly "political" songs can be startlingly effective. The beautifully eccentric lines "If you can't feed your baby/then don't have a baby" from "Wanna Be Starting Something" off the *Thriller* album remains one of my favorite examples of this. The hemistich phrasing and rhythmic structure, internal rhyming and penchant for repetition is indebted to African American preaching as well as to r&b artists like James Brown. Short, sharp, to the point; slightly left of the rest of the lyrics in this song. We rarely get long, worked out narratives, but rather quick punches that hit at gut level (there are exceptions, of course, especially in some of the ballads). They evoke, rather than describe and develop, although they can sometimes do this with incredible specificity. This technique is powerful in the context of his delivery, banal without it. *Dangerous* begins with two persuasive examples.

Jackson offers a bleak, wide lens view of human relations at the opening of this album. Both "Jam" and "Why You Wanna Trip on Me" move back and forth between the private and the public, between the harshness of the world and its effect on a single life: a powerful poetic technique and one that Jackson used often in his work. While it's difficult to avoid the conventional (and banal) reading of "Why You Wanna Trip on Me" as one of Jackson's diatribes against the tabloid press, it can also be considered, together with "Jam," as a broader reflection on the intersections between private and public, on how systemic socio-cultural problems are lived out in the everyday and how they can be eclipsed by trivialities. In fact, the lyrics in these two songs offer a pithy but trenchant critique of neoliberalism as it emerged in the 1980s, the era of Thatcher and Reagan. Neoliberalism professes that our "well-being" is best served by leaving individuals to pursue their own economic advancement. Keep rules and regulations and government to a minimum. Allow individuals to pursue "the American Dream" or whatever the other Western counterparts to this myth are. Open up markets, allow free trade. In other words, keep the state out of my economic business, loosen regulations, may the best man [sic] win. The kind of world shaped by this political ideology has been one in which the rich have gotten richer and the poor considerably poorer; it's the ideology that suggests people can fend for themselves, without a social safety net that might impinge upon "personal freedoms," and that we're all equally in a position to "pull ourselves up by the bootstraps," never mind discrepancies that come with class, race, gender, or disability.

It's an ideology that caters to those already in a position of power and privilege and works to bring even more of both into their hands. The ways in which Thatcher and Reagan, and those who have followed them have taught us to think about money has filtered down or through to the ways in which we think about most things: as David Harvey argues, "Neoliberalism has … pervasive effects on ways of thought to the point where it has become incorporated into the common-sense way many of us interpret, live in, and understand the world."[13] Jackson brings the consequences of this dogma back to intimate personal encounters between neighbors and siblings and implicates not only others in this cult of individuality and narcissism, but himself as well: I can't ask for a favor and, reciprocally, don't ask me for one either, brother: conditioned by the system, you and I are both on our own in this world that keeps changing, keeps rearranging our minds. If we're willing to consider "Tripping On Me" as meaning, broadly, a focus on the individual rather than the community, then we can also read that song as a similar kind of critique. Even if we take "me" as Jackson himself in this lyric, even if we stay with the obvious interpretation, then this reading still holds: why, Jackson asks, focus on the cult of celebrity rather than the multitude of serious problems in the world? David Brackett suggests that in songs such as "Jam" and "Man in the Mirror," songs that appear to suggest that individual agency can elicit change—or not—Jackson "ignore[s] the futility of individual action in a world where such actions are constrained by institutional and discursive forces beyond the power of any single social actor to change him- or herself or, indeed, the world."[14] Brackett articulates a key issue in neoliberalism: the ideology insists that success or failure comes down to individual agency, while the reality is that the structural barriers are far too great to allow for that. I think Jackson knew this; he doesn't use the personal exchanges in "Jam" or the "you" in "Tripping" literally, but as a means through which to understand how "the system," as he refers to it in "Jam" works on individual lives. Similarly, in "Man in the Mirror," individual agency is posited as a place to begin, not the be all and end all of change: where else *can* we begin except with a change in our own minds, with the belief that our current way of thinking is just wrong? How could we hope to act differently if we didn't start thinking differently?[15]

The world of individualism and self-importance on which Jackson focuses in these two songs recalls the fragmented surface self that characterizes postmodernity, with which neoliberalism holds a great deal in common. The equation of trying to understand "me" or "shiny celebrity" with serious issues in "Tripping" and the schizophrenic dabbling in, for example, various spiritualities—the "confusions that contradict the self" (a nice turn of phrase), the constantly changing world that "rearranges" thoughts and minds in "Jam" are symptomatic of the instability and collapse of categories that characterize postmodernity.

Now, it's easy to throw around the elastic term "postmodern" and I don't want to do it casually. Especially in the 1980s and 1990s, this was a buzzy concept that was being theorized by a number of influential scholars like Frederic Jameson, Jean-François Lyotard and Jean Baudrillard, most of them white. They wrote about the end of "master narratives," meaning ideas that universalize experience, when these were really only always about the experience of white European men. Historical narratives, the discourse of science, even fundamental Western concepts like the idea of progress all became suspect because it was clear that these were not universal but very much *situated*, in particular times and places, and relevant only to particular people. The idea that there was a single, coherent, or even rational way to understand the world came under suspicion and, frankly, just lost credibility with postmodern thinkers. All knowledge is partial and relative, "the truth" about something can never be fully known because "truth" depends on your point of view, on where you come from; those characteristics of subjectivity so centrally important to modernity—"boundedness, autonomy, interiority, depth and centrality"—are a myth. As music historian Lawrence Kramer put it, "The true human subject is fragmentary, incoherent, overdetermined, forever under construction …."[16] This de-centering discourse is what led theorists of the postmodern to talk about "difference," which allowed for voices that had not been heard before—those marginalized by race, ethnicity, gender, class—to join the conversation. It meant collapsing categories of "high" and "low" culture.

While there's much about this that can be viewed as a reason to celebrate—the de-centralization of knowledge and power is incredibly significant—this worldview also came under significant critique. Jackson's lyrics in "Jam" and "Tripping" are reminiscent of early and influential thinkers who viewed postmodernity in negative terms. Frederic Jameson, for example, wrote that postmodernism signals "the emergence of a new kind of flatness or depthlessness, a new kind of superficiality"[17] and the waning of affect (of feeling) "within fragmented postmodern selves devoid of the expressive energies characteristic of modernism."[18] Jean Baudrillard believed that representations, or simulations, of "real life" in the media were coming to replace "the real;" that we were gearing our realities to the fakes we saw on television and in the movies, like "airbrushed and digitally manipulated models in the pages of magazines, and televised re-enactments of crimes ... accepted as news stories."[19] We're so bombarded by this crap that we no longer have a sense of what's real and what's not.

But a more significant critique of the very idea that there was some *new* "fractured self" or that center/ periphery was becoming destabilized, or that the lines between "high" and "low" culture were being significantly "broken down" came from non-white scholars who knew that if you lived outside of privilege, outside of the perspective of the white intellectuals who were theorizing postmodernism, you could see that this idea was not new at all. Cornel West was one of the first black scholars to write about this, noting, in 1989, that "the sheer facticity of black people in the United States historically embodies and enacts the 'postmodern' themes of degraded otherness and subaltern marginality."[20] In other words, it's only in the privileged white imagination that a "break" occurred between the modern and the postmodern. Similarly, bell hooks wrote in the early 1990s of the "exclusionary" nature of postmodernist discourses, with few African American scholars taking part in the debate about difference, otherness, or the decentering of culture from the dominant white, European and male modernist traditions, even as African

Americans and other minority cultures were the subject of these debates.[21] Michele Wallace, writing specifically about Jackson, commented:

> The past for Afro-American culture, particularly that oral tradition … pursued by the black masses has been precisely a postmodern one … . It should thus come as no surprise when the telltale 'schizophrenia' and 'pastiche' of postmodernism are considered by some black artists to be characteristic of the enemy within, or racism internalized. In contrast, the most enlightened trends in contemporary Afro-American culture are in consistent pursuit of meaning, history, continuity, and the power of subjectivity. I am calling these various heterogeneous, and sometimes conflicting efforts Black Modernisms, of which Jackson's recent performance is perhaps a new type.[22]

Cornel West, bell hooks, Michele Wallace and others view music as a primary means through which African Americans have expressed ideas about their marginality, and hooks sites rap as having "usurped the primary position of rhythm and blues music among young black folks" as a means through which they can "develop a critical voice," "a form of 'testimony' for the under-class."[23] This may have been true when she was writing, but r&b and hybrid r&b/rap styles have continued as a powerful forum for the expression of the politics of the marginalized.

While Jackson's art and public life can absolutely be considered "postmodern," indeed, even "posthuman" (see Chapter 4) in its various transgressions of "the normal," at the beginning of *Dangerous*, Jackson is wary of the fractured postmodern self. As Wallace writes, he is terrorized by the loss of meaning, history, continuity, and subjectivity. He worries about the debilitating effects of decentering, disengaging, disconnecting, of losing a sense of belonging and responsibility towards each other. Rather than celebrating, Jackson, like scholars such as West and hooks, seems "suspicious of postmodern critiques of the 'subject' when these appear at the precise moment when many minorities felt that, for the first time, they had a voice and could speak openly about their experiences."[24]

Jackson uses the fractured postmodern self as a foil against which to moralize in "Tripping" and there what he can mostly do is name the problems, ask a question and demand it stop; but in "Jam" he moves to a solution and it's an interesting one to ponder. "Jamming" in its broadest sense means to engage, to act, and, in most cases, to form community in the process.[25] It means making music with others who are, if not strangers, then those with whom one does not normally "play." These are informal associations, loose, casual, improvisatory. It suggests the creation of temporary but perhaps deeply meaningful and productive alliances with strangers. Heavy D's verse on this song is a commentary on the process of jamming *with* Jackson (making funky tracks with Mike, who's so relaxed), his crafty "move up" from fan to fellow musician, and his previous jams with sister Janet and the hip hop group Guy. Jackson's point is that no matter how screwed up the world is, it's never too screwed up to be creative. The second time we hear Heavy D, his rap has been reduced to a mantra: "It ain't too hard for me to jam," which is simply repeated over and over again, the repetition keeping us in the present moment and serving as a kind of rehearsal of the power of jamming. I'm still always taken aback by this moment in the song, when all of the complex rhythmic movement and the noisiness of the instrumental sounds momentarily give way to what is, after all, a chant, almost a prayer.

Jamming can be taken as a metaphor in this context, for coming together to create *anything* in a positive way. *Acting* is, in and of itself, powerful, transgressive. But jamming is an idea that is specifically rooted in vernacular culture: Jackson locates a solution not through structured politics, institutions, or the powerful. This idea ties in with the postmodern, especially with black theorists who point to vernacular artistic traditions as politically subversive. Jackson also means for solutions to be embodied—this is not an intellectual exercise, but one that engages the body creatively. The word "Jam" has been used in a wide variety of musical contexts, including its probable origin in jazz and its subsequent use in rock music of the 1960s, not only to describe "jam bands," like the Grateful Dead, but in the powerful phrase "Kick Out the Jams, Motherfucker," that opened the MC5's album, widely taken to be a middle finger to authority. But the term was everywhere in hip hop culture in the 1980s. There, it was often used to refer to a DJ's mix, a jam of potentially contradictory styles and sounds. Influential DJs incorporated the term into their monikers, including Run DMC's Jam Master Jay and Jimmy Jam (with whom Jackson worked on the *Dangerous* album). The influential and now-legendary hip hop label Def Jam Records chose to define themselves through this idea. It's probable that Bob Marley's influential 1977 song "Jammin'" played a role in the use of this term in hip hop culture; in fact, lyrically, Jackson's "Jam" has quite a bit in common with Marley's classic, also about the idea of jamming as a salve to world weariness and a rallying cry to action, equally fragmented in the images it offers and in the insistent repetition of the core idea: "we're jammin'." Important for Jackson the dancer is that jamming is also a central idea in b-boy/girl culture: b-boy competitions are called jams, and going head to head with another dancer is called jamming. And so Jackson situates himself fully within the world of hip hop as action, *as resistance*: this is where a considerable part of the politics of this song lies. The lyrics of "Jam" can, in fact, be viewed as a kind of meta-text on the crucial role of hip hop in contemporary culture: as a creative means through which dissent is expressed and community created. Of course the cynical view would be that "Jam" just reiterates Jackson's oft-stated position that he himself used art as a retreat—the stage was, as he said many times, the place where he felt most comfortable. But that interpretation belongs a) to those who don't think that creativity—of any kind, let alone creativity that manifests through the body—is a powerful form of agency, b) to those who don't think that jamming can, in addition to granting agency and creating community, offer critique on the state of the world and c) to those who'd rather not think too deeply about Jackson's work.

Opening the record—and the live show—with this song was a way to point to the act of creating music, so that all the songs that follow are grasped as belonging to the *process*, as a series of case studies: it ain't too hard for me to jam—watch me do it in this and the next 13 songs, or in the live show, watch me do it for the next two hours. In this respect, *Dangerous* follows in the footsteps of The Beatles' *Sgt. Pepper's* album, the first song of which also frames the record as a performance—"hope you will enjoy the show." In fact the counting off ("1, 2, 3") at the beginning of "Jam" strengthens the connection to *Sgt. Pepper's*, even if Paul McCartney's crisp counting off comes not in the opening, but in the reprise of the title track to that album.

*   *   *

The short film for "Jam" makes explicit the links between jamming, agency and community—specifically the black community—and so connects back to the black critique of postmodernism. "Black or White" was the lead single off the album and although there were others released in between it and "Jam," there are interesting parallels between these two films. Both films put race front and center, but from quite different perspectives: overtly—for the benefit of a white audience—in "Black or White," and more covertly, through location, the presence of children and celebrities of color, and through the vernacular in "Jam." "Black or White" begins with the camera zooming down into a suburban neighborhood at night, where white families are tucked away in their pristine homes; no one's on the street. At the beginning of "Jam," the camera moves through the inner city, first in slow motion, past a "no parking" sign—who's not welcome here?—and then, once the globe breaks through the window and hits the ground, it moves at breakneck speed, at street level, through an inner city wasteland. It's daytime and kids are on these streets, not in tidy homes; all of them are black (there's only one white child featured in this film, and it's a relatively brief shot; he's imitating Jackson's iconic dance moves while Jackson looks on). The kids do what's available for them to do: one dances, one bounces up and down on an old chair, some skip rope. But many just stand, their faces emerging from the shadows, looking purposefully into the camera, in the way that Jackson does in his "panther dance" in "Black or White"—those who are usually surveilled and held in suspicion look back.

The scene shifts to Jackson, inside one of the old buildings, dancing; he delivers most of the first verse in profile silhouette. Eventually there's also a shot of Michael Jordan in silhouette. These silhouettes could belong to no one other than Michael Jackson and Michael Jordan—the two MJs who dominated the world of music and sports at the time, the stature of their celebrity so great, their images so iconic, that they could be represented without the specific physical details required for the recognition of mere mortals. Jackson and Jordan are *doing* from the moment we see them. They are active, engaged, they're jamming. It's this doing that has catapulted them, black men, the subjugated, into stratospheric success. Throughout the film, the kids become increasingly engaged, playing music, sports, and dancing. Jackson and Jordan are shown as virtuosos in their respective fields, but they also move out of their comfort zones, Jackson trying his hand at basketball, Jordan at dancing—their awkwardness is funny, but there's also a lesson about joining in, taking a leap of faith, and creating community. As Armond White put it, "Jam" is a political statement, where the "typical routes of black achievement" are viewed as reveling in "the glory of the moment, the brotherly communion." The bodies in the film are playing games, "but plainly, the world is at stake."[26]

* * *

If it weren't for the specific, powerful ways in which individual songs are put together, none of this would really matter. You can talk about jamming, or use noise on your record, or write some lyrics about the pitiful state of the world, but unless these come together through convincing music, unless the performances pack a punch, no one's going to care. People care about Jackson's music and dance because he was such a magnificent craftsman and he surrounded himself with other highly accomplished musicians—yet there's precious little detailed analysis of his songs. What makes "Jam" a particularly persuasive document about the neoliberal subject or the condition of postmodernity lies, largely, in the sound and in Jackson's performance; his tortured voice and the way in which formal elements of the music are deployed are equally, if not more, significant than the lyrics. Or maybe we can just say that they work together brilliantly.

It's almost a full minute before Jackson begins to sing. That's a long time for a pop song and we have to ask, what's the purpose of this intro, what's its effect? In the *This Is It* documentary, Jackson says to his band twice when rehearsing "The Way You Make Me Feel" how important it is to stay in the moment, to pause before moving on, to repeat an eight-bar pattern one more time. "You have to be totally nourished by it," he says, "You gotta let it simmer, just bathe in the moonlight." Especially on his later records, when, I suspect, he didn't have Quincy Jones reigning in his excess, he loved to let the music "simmer"—lengthy intros, endless repetition of choruses. This is what happens in the long opening of "Jam." Get into that groove, let it develop, let your body feel it fully before starting to sing. An 8-bar pattern is repeated three times in this intro and the element that's most highlighted is the turntable scratching that often articulates the fourth of a group of four beats—a signature sound of hip hop dominates the musical landscape from the outset. You have to listen hard, but there's another nod to hip hop in this introduction: on the sixth beat of the second and third groups of eight, there's an interjection of a sound dissonant to the rest of the texture; much more subtle than one would find in the music of, say Public Enemy (where such a high-pitched dissonant sound often occurs on the backbeat), but it is there, in homage, nonetheless. This dissonance is part of the noisiness, part of the disruptive character of lots of early rap.

It's not as though the voice is absent from this introduction. Right from the count off, we hear an electronically-manipulated voice (Jackson's or Riley's?), a cyborgian voice, baiting the listener: you wanna get up and jam? The fluidity of this voice, its state of flux—high, low, human, machine—is classic Jackson: we don't only get his love of mutability and transformation in visual form (werewolf, zombie, panther), but through the countless ways he changes his voice from song to song and even within songs. It sounds as though his cyborg representation on the album cover is slowly coming to life (see Chapter 4). We also hear Jackson's breath. As the third iteration of the 8-bar pattern begins, it's not unreasonable to assume he's going to start singing: instead, his sharp expulsion of air comes down hard on the third beat of the bar. The long lead-up to this point has allowed Jackson to immerse himself in the groove; he's already engulfed by it, physically inside of it, responding to it from deep within his body, inhabiting it as he always did in his music. It's exquisite to hear his intensity, this intimacy, to hear the human body laboring, especially juxtaposed with the laid back machine-manipulated voice.

When Jackson does begin to sing he sounds terrified and wounded. He's used this voice before—it's reminiscent of the way he sang parts of "Billie Jean" and "Dirty Diana," a sense that he might collapse into tears at any moment—but the intensity is of a different kind here and there are a number of good musical reasons for that. The melody is like a run-on sentence and it sounds as if Jackson won't have enough breath to get through it—sometimes he just barely makes it to the end of a phrase. And although the rhythm of this melody is made up of straight eighth notes (no swingin'), they're all sung ahead of the beat, like he can't wait, he's in too much of a rush, or maybe even panic, to stay in synch with the music. Adding to the tension is the fact that there's very little bottom end in the verses— it feels like we're in suspension. While the bass hits hard on every other downbeat during the introduction and the choruses, it's absent from the verses. This makes them seem ungrounded, and because the bass sound is so fat in the intro and chorus, its immediate withdrawal seems to pull up the ground from underneath. In fact the bass guitar is used incredibly sparingly throughout the whole song, eventually coming in, walking style, only to prepare the downbeat during the choruses, with a little more sustained use in the outro. It's a technique that Jackson uses more than once on this album to give a sense of ungroundedness. On top of all that, his anguished vocal is mirrored (not quite doubled) by a keyboard line played an octave above where he's singing, which intensifies the drama of his vocal; this drops out during the choruses, where a more relaxed mid-range keyboard part takes over. The character of verse and chorus are completely different and that's because the problem is laid out in the verses, whereas a solution is offered in the chorus. The verses follow the formal shape of the blues, tapping into that long and deep musical tradition. I know the form has been so ubiquitous in pop music that its use hardly seems significant to point out, but this *is* a lament, isn't it, so what better form to use? Jackson liked to reference the blues overtly in his laments on the state of the world: it's also his language of choice for the long, cathartic ending of "Earth Song."

Jackson kicks up the tension in the melody by diving in on an unstable note, a dissonance (C), hammering it into our heads before offering a little resolution by dropping down a pitch (to B); traditional blues melodies descend like this—it's part of their lamenting quality. Jackson's choice to endlessly repeat a single pitch in the chorus is also interesting. It's all about rhythm, about him using his voice as a percussion instrument, contributing to the groove rather than creating a more conventional melody. Although Jackson was a great singer even as a child, I'd argue that he became greater as he got older, always developing new ways to use his voice, changing its character with each song. In "Jam" he takes his cue from James Brown. In fact, this song is a full-on tribute to Brown, what with Jackson's clipped and distorted singing style in the chorus, the retro horns, the overwhelming significance of "the One," Brown's insistence that, no matter how rhythmically complicated things got in between, everyone would come together on the downbeat. There was a lot of homage being paid to Brown in hip hop, but Jackson had always paid tribute. Here he makes it even more explicit than he had before.

The character of Jackson's voice changes drastically from verse to chorus. The woundedness and angst—and the clean timbre and heavy vibrato—give way to a choked up, stuttering, and distorted sound the likes of which we've never heard from Jackson before, especially by the end of the track. This is decidedly *not* the voice of a "man-child" as people liked to (condescendingly) call Jackson, nor is it the voice of someone who "wanted to be white." It's the voice of an adult man who understood and was deeply connected to his black musical roots. Given his upbringing among r&b greats like Brown and Jackie Wilson, he always had a tendency to "go raw," as Nelson George has expressed it,[27] but this tendency grew more pronounced in his later works, starting here; there's less and less of that pristine, conventionally beautiful tenor and more grit and roughness. More blackness. More machismo. More man with a point of view. More noise. More danger.

Desire

Michael Jackson's diffuse expression of sexuality, which so many people have found disturbing, because it doesn't fit into any normative paradigm, is the 'line of flight' along which he continued to singularize himself … . [It] is the aspect of his persona, or expression, that is least understood today, and that desperately needs to be more fully explored. Steven Shapiro

Some of the cruelest and most dehumanizing things that have been said about Michael Jackson have to do with gender and sexuality, so in trying to tell new stories about him, I feel compelled to begin a chapter called "Desire" with fans' voices; critics should listen. If you go to YouTube and search "Michael Jackson Sexy" (it was a late night; one link led to another), the number of fan photo and video montages that come up is mindboggling. Most of them are comprised entirely of images from the "Bad" years or later, from when he was a grown, increasingly gender ambiguous man. Some, like the nearly five-minute long "Michael Jackson sexy very hot!"[1] focus on his final years, including a long opening shot of Jackson at the MTV Video Awards in Japan, 2006, the camera slowly scanning his body from the boots up. Among the gushing comments made by some of the seventy thousand or so viewers is this: "40-50 years old is his sexiest period." It's not an uncommon sentiment, along with others that proclaim, "I love looking at this man! So sexy, so beautiful, so amazing." Or: "Sexiest man in the world, undisputed." The creator of one such video asks viewers, "Hey ladies, can you imagine how is to having sex with Michael Jackson?" The labored English suggests that maybe videos and sentiments such as these belong to fans outside of North America, in areas of the world that have less stultifying views on gender and sexuality, but I'm not sure about that; plenty of the comments do English just fine. There are all kinds of posts on Twitter proclaiming Jackson's hotness, complete with pictures. There's also artwork, such as the Photoshopped images by Gella De which depict an often latter-day Jackson and the artist as lovers.[2] Even Madonna said in a 2009 interview in *Rolling Stone*, "I was madly in love with him, totally smitten … . The songs he sang were not childlike at all."[3]

With all the talk of how Jackson "destroyed" his face and became a monster in his later years, often described as "an inevitable tragedy to pity and mourn,"[4] it's interesting to contemplate this very different discourse. What do these fans find so sexy, so beautiful, when pretty much all we hear from the media is that he was a freak? Some critics have admitted that Jackson "[irradiated] sexual dynamism"[5] in his performances, but then they've knocked the wind out of that claim by determining that it was all show and no action: "He might be threatening if Jackson gave, even for a second, the impression that he is obtainable,"[6] wrote Jay Cocks in 1984. Since when did the obtainability of pop stars have anything to do with them as threatening to society's mores? Mark Fisher wrote off the short film for "The Way You Make Me Feel" by declaring, "as if the increasingly absurd performance of peacock-posturing intimidation substitutes for any actual sexual desire;"[7] I'd like to know what "actual" means here. Margo Jefferson concluded that "Michael Jackson, the performer, has never offered portraits of black or white masculinity that are at all realistic or, better, conventional."[8] The latter is true; how it's parallel to the former is a mystery. And what is "realistic" masculinity? Reid Kane concluded that Jackson's masculinity was "feigned."[9] I could go on at considerable length citing sources that are variations on this theme, but you get the point.

For many, the sexualized performances Jackson gave in his short films and on stage were too stylized to be believed and they required authentication through "real life" experience; he needed to validate, to *prove* that those thrusting hips, the hand gliding sensuously down his chest, fingers stroking his groin while he closed his eyes and caught his breath were more than theatrics, more than shuck and jive—where was his girlfriend? Or boyfriend? Why was he so shy and soft-spoken off the stage? Right, he must be asexual, or gay, or "pre-sexual," as Randall Sullivan has weirdly tagged it, labels applied either with scorn or with the intention of pathologizing Jackson's sexuality.[10] These ways of looking at him make a number of questionable suppositions. For instance, that the stylized performance of sexuality isn't "believable" and therefore couldn't be "threatening." If this were true, there would have been no uproar about Elvis. Artistic performance is extremely powerful, can be life-changing for those who view or listen to it, can create a world that folks can dream about or act upon, can awaken ideas about love, romance and sex that we hadn't thought possible before. Jackson created a sexualized presence on stage that is as real as it gets in that moment—he knew exactly how to conjure up a powerfully erotic body, just like so many performers do; and just as those other performers elicit "real" emotional responses from their fans, so did Jackson. In fact, what sets Jackson apart is that he positively *wrung* feeling out of his performances; both his voice and body dripped with passion, pulling us into a world of sensuality so vibrant, so intense, impossible for most of the rest of us to express, or maybe even feel. He modeled it *for* us and to show us that it was possible to burn this brightly. How couldn't you be mesmerized? How couldn't some feel threatened?

Critics also suppose that this performance must be carried over into everyday life, otherwise it's being faked, and that you can't be both soft-spoken and shy in one context and radiate "sexual dynamism" in another. Regardless of what we know about his private sexual life, he radiated, even when he was being soft-spoken: all that sexual energy didn't just dissipate when he left the stage. And I'd say it's precisely the combination of "softness" with erotic "dynamism" that leads fans to think he was the "most sexy man ever;" this combination is a dream come true, people, an elusive but highly sought after blend of characteristics fantasized about by, at least, straight girls all over the world.

But there's good reason for all this poo-pooing of

Jackson's powerful sexual energy: denying it and his masculinity, as well as his maturity, which terms like the omnipresent "man-child" do,[11] demanding reconciliation between his on- and off-stage performances of sexuality and concluding that he became grotesque and therefore undesirable through plastic surgery, works to contain his complex gendered and sexualized self and to police the boundaries of what can be considered desirable, sexy, and masculine. It erases the beautiful conundrum. But it also makes him safer.

*   *   *

Jackson gives us four different views of love near the beginning of *Dangerous*, grouping together the lustful "In the Closet" and "She Drives Me Wild," with the nostalgic "Remember the Time," and the nervous "Can't Let Her Get Away." It's a full-on assault of all things sensual, sexual, and romantic like we haven't seen from him before. While so much of his music appeals across generations, these songs break away from that; the adult sentiments don't, significantly for Jackson, speak to children or, perhaps, to older fans (like my 87-year-old neighbor, who listens to Jackson's music all the time, but only through the *Bad* album, not later work). All in all, these songs suggest that love is complicated and cruel—he's chasing it (her), but can't quite get it; he had it, but it slips away; he's got it—he's got it bad—but it needs to be hidden. These songs are as much about desires of the flesh as those of the heart, a direction that Jackson had explored earlier in more cinematic ways, in songs like "Billie Jean" and "Dirty Diana." But the songs on *Dangerous* feel more personal, more in the moment, more about a guy who's wrestling with his libido and his heart. And unlike those earlier *femme fatale* songs, or sentimental ballads about romantic love, Jackson is a willing partner, turned on, if never quite getting what he wants or needs. Isn't that how the most powerful love songs go? While Robert Christgau thought Jackson was "hawking the most credible sex-and-romance of his career" on *Dangerous*,[12] Jon Pareles found this adult Jackson so improbable that he wrote in his review of the record: "of all the bizarre apparitions in current popular music, none is stranger than Michael Jackson singing ordinary love songs. He can barely choke them out … [they] sound like they're being extracted under torture … his songs proclaim a terror of the body and of fleshly pleasures."[13]

Pareles was just dead wrong. What Jackson taps into in these songs is the long tradition of what Mark Anthony Neal calls "soul man" masculinity, no doubt influenced by, or perhaps even a response to, the resurgence of "harder, more 'street,' or 'authentic' versions of blackness" as cultivated in hip hop and perhaps also the hard-edged masculinity of metal.[14] Jackson managed a version of gritty masculinity that maintained gender ambivalence and that was not, on the whole, violent or misogynistic. His reclamation of soul man masculinity made sense for him, since he repeatedly claimed that musical tradition, thought it to be where his musical roots lay. Cultivated in the 1960s in the midst of the Black Power Movement, soul men such as Sam Cooke, Marvin Gaye, Solomon Burke, James Brown, and Wilson Pickett, "captured," Neal explains, "the imagination of black America during an era when hyperblack, hyper-masculine, hypersexual male icons seemed logical retorts to ongoing ideological threats centered on notions of American masculinity."[15] This performance of black masculinity at this particular historical moment acted as a shield from the long tradition of the white emasculation of black men, as well as their general dehumanization; soul performers such as these were, as Neal observes, the musical equivalents of Malcolm X and Eldridge Cleaver. Neal suggests that Jackson's drive to be a best-selling commercial artist led him away from this conventional performance of black masculinity and towards one that could be considered "queer" in that it challenged the stereotypes and made Jackson seem "safe" for young white consumers and their parents.[16] After all, while it may have been an important recuperative strategy for black men to construct themselves as hypermasculine in the 1960s and later, it was also risky, since there was the long racist tradition of reductively viewing them as hypersexualized—as sex and nothing else, and threatening because of it. Eddie Murphy made the point about Jackson's careful negotiation of black masculinity bluntly back in the 1980s:[17]

> Michael's so famous. Everything he says the public believes. He went on television and said "I don't have sex because of my religious beliefs" and the public believed it. Brothers were like "get the fuck out of here" and white people going "that Michael's a special kind of guy, he's good, clean and wholesome." Y'all believed [what he said]. You know how y'all believed it? Y'all didn't get mad when he took Brooke Shields to the Grammy's; nobody

white said shit. And Brooke Shields is the whitest woman in America … . If I took Brooke Shields to the Grammy's y'all would lose your minds.

So there was, certainly, a strategy behind Jackson's self-presentation as shy, humble, respectful, and disinterested in sex off stage. Soul men didn't achieve the kind of mainstream success that MJ did. But with *Dangerous* he started taking greater risks, offering songs that deal more explicitly with sex, cultivating a raunchier singing style, and presenting himself as more sexualized in his public appearances: out with the risky Madonna at the Oscars, for instance, or in his short film for "In the Closet" with Naomi Campbell, in his steamy photo shoot with Herb Ritts, and on stage. He revived and transformed soul man masculinity and played it against signifiers that were way outside its range: he mashed up traditional machismo with high femme glamor and soft-spoken sensitivity. The machismo was mapped on to an androgynous look that, because he *was* getting older, became increasingly aligned with that of an adult woman more than his earlier youthful lad look. It's not surprising that this turn wreaked havoc with his "good boy" image and started moving him, for some, into murkier and scarier gendered territory.

*   *   *

The first time that noise gives way on *Dangerous* is at the beginning of "In the Closet;" the calm doesn't last for long. The opening strains of the song, anchored by acoustic piano but unfolding into a symphonic drama with warp speed, is timbrally and rhythmically softer than anything we've heard up to this point and, because it's the music that frames the "Mystery Girl's" narrative of longing and desire, lends itself to being aligned with the feminine, as softer, quieter music often has been (the "Mystery Girl," so identified in the liner notes, turned out to be Princess Stephanie of Monaco). Each time the girl speaks throughout the song, we hear remnants of this opening music, suspending the groove and the song's normal progression through time. The juxtaposition of this music with another hard, noisy, industrial groove that finds Jackson wary of divulging what lovers say or do continues the caution and skepticism found in the opening two songs of the album; public and private worlds are also juxtaposed here but musically that's not accomplished simply by contrasting the girl's music with Jackson's (too easy). His hard groove heard in the verses creates a private realm of exquisite tension, of desire that churns and smolders while still (barely) remaining undercover—you can hear it wanting to boil over. The tension finds a home in the main riff, which centers around a half step, the smallest interval possible in tonal music; Jackson's melody is confined to only four notes. The backing harmonies are dense, bunched up, intervallically constricted, and mirror the back and forth movement of the riff; they are so compressed that they sound like they're coming from inside a vacuum (or perhaps a closet).

The thing is, these musical characteristics also sound conventionally "exotic" to Western ears. Jackson's melody is formed out of a pentatonic (five note) scale—it's often used in the blues, but here it sounds "Eastern," because of the way it's heard within the context of the half-step riff. The parallel motion of the backing vocals, separated by the interval of a fourth, is uncharacteristic of modern Western music. And the reverberating timbre of the drum on the downbeat sounds more related to Middle-Eastern than r&b grooves. This cramped music opens up during the chorus, where we get a proper bass line (absent in the verses and just as with "Jam" this creates a feeling of rootlessness) and Jackson soars up an octave, the breathy whisper of his voice giving way to falsetto ecstasy. This chorus collapses twice just, it seems, as it's about to take off—aborted attempts at fulfillment, joy, release. The third time the music of the chorus takes flight and is allowed to develop, to "simmer." Jackson's repeated ad libs culminate in his trademark "hee hee," signifying here in a profoundly different way than it ever has before—as surrender, capitulation, and fulfillment: usually this vocal gesture comes as a sharp interjection, all bravado, control, affirmation of the music's energy and power. Here, it rounds out his series of ad libs, using his last bit of breath: a haunting, the release of a former, younger self. Rather than fading out on the chorus, suggesting this blissful state might go on forever, the song ends back *in* the closet, back in the private world of conspiratorial whispers, confining music and slamming doors, but also, without a doubt, of heated passion: oh, there's passion in this closet, make no mistake. Breaking glass, which we've also heard at the beginning of the second verse, reappears here: this relationship is about testing boundaries, about wanting to break free of social constraints, but in what sense?

People were understandably puzzled by Jackson's use

of the expression "in the closet" to characterize a straight relationship and one has to admit that this is tantalizingly confusing, more so because in a way, this is a kind of "coming out" song for Jackson even as he's talking, ambiguously, about keeping things in the closet—coming out, that is, as interested not only in romance but sex, as a willing, even aggressive participant, not betrayed by and fearful of some *femme fatale* and, unbelievably to some, as straight. And in the short films for "In the Closet," and "Remember the Time," his interaction with the women is front and center (as it also was in "The Way You Make Me Feel," probably his first foray into soul man masculinity), even though some concluded that he "fails" at these interactions; I sometimes wonder whether I'm watching the same films as the critics. Maybe the subtext of "In the Closet" was to let us know that, despite prevalent media views to the contrary, he'd always been interested in sex and had just been very good at keeping his interest hidden as part of his desire to reach a large, white, audience, to mythologize himself and to challenge normative ideas of how masculinity can be performed (as in, he didn't need a posse of good-looking women around him to prove his straightness—he didn't need to use women in that way). At least we can make these speculations when listening to the audio alone; in the short film, Jackson wears a wedding ring, which makes it pretty clear that the narrative is about adultery that needs to be kept under wraps. Gee, that's a pretty grown-up subject.

The musical language of "In the Closet" could easily be viewed as problematically exoticizing the sexual in a way that plays into white Western, Orientalist stereotypes of mysterious, alluring otherness. And maybe that's what it is: why cast the most sexually-explicit song of your career in the trappings of non-Western musical sounds that evoke those stereotypes? The problem with this interpretation is that Jackson doesn't speak from within the dominant culture—*he* is the racial/ethnic other, the androgyne; he is difference. He is the "exotic" other that the music helps establish, the alluring subject that is desired. At least this is how we might be able to think about it when listening to the song; again, the short film gives us another narrative. Often in Orientalist fantasies it's the dark-skinned woman who's exoticized, who's portrayed as some kind of "forbidden fruit," and Naomi Campbell is so dark next to Jackson that he might be thought of as racially other to her, a potentially controversial idea, I know, given that Jackson's increasingly lighter skin led to him sometimes being called a "race traitor." I don't mean to buy into those narratives here: only that there appears to be, on the level of skin color, a substantial racial difference between Jackson and Campbell, and that Campbell is treated as a hyper-sexualized "exotic" woman of color in this film in a way that plays right into the stereotypes.[18] The location and setting for the film is also intended to play on this idea of the exotic: Ritts said that he wanted a "Spanish kind of exotic woman," for the film[19] and others have noted the "Spanish" elements of the set (the women's clothing, for example) and Jackson's "Paso Doble"-like dance moves.[20] The question is why (I'm afraid I have no answer: did Ritts understand he was buying into an Orientalist fantasy? Did Michael?)

*   *   *

In these "machismo" songs, it's not torture or fear we're getting in Jackson's voice, it's the fierceness of James Brown or Wilson Pickett: think "Mustang Sally" when you listen to "She Drives me Wild" and parts of "Can't Let Her Get Away;" it's the smooth, impossibly high falsetto that Neal argues the soul man uses to seduce, a marker of hypermasculinity that signals his mastery of style.[21] Compare Marvin Gaye's "Trouble Man" to "In the Closet." Jackson's voice is breathier, but even the phrasing in the two songs is strikingly similar. And it's the warm, fluid tenor of a singer like Sam Cooke—think "You Send Me" when you listen to the relaxed tenor in the verses of "Remember the Time," the smoothest Jackson has sounded so far on this record. Jackson's voice has a lighter quality than that of these men—and that's what makes gendered meaning significantly different in his voice: he doesn't possess the same heaviness, the depth. Except for "In the Closet," these songs are pitched slightly below and above middle C—that's the range in which Pickett sings "Mustang Sally," but his voice sounds fuller, heavier and more conventionally masculine than Jackson's. Even so, Jackson's timbre and his clipped and guttural singing style later in his career make his voice legible as "masculine."[22] But the emotional landscape that Jackson paints—in almost all of his songs—is more intense and extreme than most soul man singers and this can quite easily be gendered as "feminine," as borrowing from soul divas like Patti Labelle or Diana Ross. As Jacqueline Warwick writes, "[a]s an adult singer, Jackson famously adopted many of Diana Ross's vocal mannerisms, such as her trick of punctuating a phrase with a graceful portamento sigh or a squeak."[23] Think of Jackson's weepy pleas to "dare me" to "keep it in the closet." It's in part this combination of gendered styles and specific characteristics of singing that makes Jackson's performances "confusing." The visual, of course, adds another dimension to this ambiguity.

I've wanted to dwell on how Jackson's performances line up with conventional masculinity because this is mostly overlooked or denied in commentary on his gender. Even in his visual appearance and performance, there's plenty that fits within the realm of the masculine—including his tough-guy gangster persona—but in order to understand that, it's important to focus on the details *at specific times in his career* (you can't talk about it all in one fell swoop). During the *Dangerous* era, Jackson started wearing his hair longer and more loosely curled. The jheri curl had morphed into several strands that often hung over his eyes and reached his chin. It's during this time that he also first straightens, rather than relaxes, his hair (as in the short film for "Remember the Time"). As he ages, from *Dangerous* onward, his face becomes increasingly "feminized," exaggerated through the use of make-up, including heavy eyeliner, mascara and various shades of lipstick—earlier in his career his use of make-up was less heavy-handed. There's a tendency to put all of Jackson's various looks down to surgery that created structural changes, but as Willa Stillwater argues, make-up, lighting and the aging process must also be taken into account. Stillwater suggests that the media went out of their way in later years to choose unflattering photographs of Jackson, to make him look more "hideous."[24] Meredith Jones makes the compelling argument that Jackson's facial features marked him as "intergender" because he incorporated—side by side—signifiers of both conventional masculinity and femininity. His wide, made-up eyes and small, thin nose by the time of *Dangerous* read as conventionally feminine (the changes to his nose were not only about race), while his relatively wide, cleft chin reads as masculine.[25] He was always clean shaven during this time period (he occasionally sported facial hair—around the time of *Thriller*, and again in 2001, for example), but he always wore prominent sideburns. This analytical specificity begins to get at how Jackson's intriguing performance of gender really works: the features don't "add up" to one gender or another, nor can they be "reconciled." Markers of masculinity do not disappear. In fact these characteristics, particularly the square jaw-line and cleft chin, became more pronounced as he aged, perhaps through procedures, perhaps through fluctuating weight, or perhaps, again, simply through the natural process of aging.

But we have to go beyond his face and hair to get at Jackson's ambiguous performance of gender. His body was slight, without developed muscles, but straight, angular and strong—not a feminine thing about it, including the way he moved, right down to his walk. When he ripped away his t-shirt in some performances and bared his chest, like he does in the "panther dance" at the end of "Black or White," a perfectly smooth and adolescent upper body is revealed. In his costume for the *Dangerous* tour, however, the gold fencing shirt drew attention to his bulging groin; his stylist Michael Bush commented, rightly, that this piece "left very little to the imagination."[26] His dancing was very often hard, controlled, and angular as well: those pelvic thrusts, for example, or his crotch grabs.

Margo Jefferson thought these were about reminding us that he's "a man. A Black man."[27] Possibly, since he so often wasn't considered to be one. But they weren't ever really "grabs" so much as a stylized and often downright elegant gesturings *towards*. Working with dancers in *This Is It* to try to get the movement just right, one of the choreographers says "I don't think it's anything but hand movement, do you know what I mean?" (in other words, you don't clutch and move your stuff, as the dancers wanted to do). Jefferson calls the move "desperate," but on the basis of what? Those moves are controlled, deliberate, flirtatious, *daring*. It's a provocation. In addition to the idea that Jackson is "making a statement about who he is in the face of endless scrutiny and interrogation regarding his blackness, his masculinity, and his sexuality," Joe Vogel adds that he is also "protesting the cruel history of mutilation by flaunting the symbol of his creative power and identity as a black man. No one, he suggests … can prevent him from doing it."[28] In the short film for "Jam," he makes the move just before there's a break in the music; at the break, he looks into the camera with a small inhalation of breath and raised eyebrows in a mock apology: "Oops, I didn't mean to, but I just can't help myself. Sorry, did I offend you? Good. Piss off."

But the gesture could also be more ambiguous, more unsettling. In the "panther dance" the crotch "grab" becomes a rub—sometimes he only uses his middle finger; and he rubs his hand down his chest into his groin too. All this rubbing, if we have to bring things down to conventional binaries, is much more associated with female masturbation, less with jerking off. Not that this cuts Jackson much of a break: not only is it feminized, but masturbation has long been associated with deviance and shame, which is how it was read in the "panther dance."[29] "He needs to get married, quick," was the comment made by a viewer who called into a radio station the day after the premiere of "Black or White," and dutifully reported in *Entertainment Weekly*.[30] It's clearly too much to see a man pleasuring himself, period, let alone using gestures that are associated with the feminine: if masturbation has historically been shameful for men, it's been even more so for women.

I'm wary of trying to label Jackson's performance of gender and sexuality because his idea, as I see it, was to get us to question—especially to question the parameters of masculinity and heterosexuality (he insisted he was straight and there's no evidence he wasn't)—without necessarily settling. Using terms like "queer" (which I've done to describe his musical practices, a different thing entirely) or "trans" becomes quite problematic in this context (unless we're willing to use "queer" in its broadest possible sense) and in any case, I'm not sure how far those terms get us, "trans" in particular (he didn't "cross over").[31] I do, however, like Judith Peraino's phrase "coming out into the middle," which she uses in her discussion of androgyny. Peraino takes this discussion back to the eighteenth century and the writings of the influential Enlightenment historian Johann Winckelmann, who as a good neoclassicist believed in the importance of "balance," that beauty was "nothing other than the middle between two extremes," a position he came to through his study of classical Greek and Roman statues (Jackson himself had these sprinkled around the grounds of Neverland Ranch). Winckelmann "was fascinated with the indeterminate genders of the ancient statues; he believed [they] presented, to the keen observer, examples of dynamic metamorphosis." The "middle way" was not "a careful path" for Winckelmann: not "a means for avoiding danger or conflict." It was, indeed, "a path that emerged from passion and confrontation."[32] This is why it is at once alluring and frightening, the instability captivating and, to some, horrifying—especially if one moves, as Winckelmann did in his observations, from the fictive world of ancient statuary into the real world of androgynous masculinity.

*　　*　　*

"Remember the Time" is not the first instance of Jackson invoking Africa in his work. The song "Liberian Girl" was lauded by Nelson George, among others, as one of the first to celebrate black female beauty in Western pop culture.[33] The short film for "Remember" offered a vehicle through which an image of black power, wealth, and opulence could be showcased; we're remembering not only a love relationship in the film, but a moment at which Africa was a center of power. It was intended as a reminder, at a moment when black poverty and disempowerment were predominant images circulating in American culture—this film was made in the wake of the Rodney King beatings, the white police officers' acquittal, and the Los Angeles riots that ensued—that things once were and perhaps could again be different. John Singleton, who had in the previous year directed the critically-acclaimed film *Boyz N the Hood*, asked Jackson if he could hire an all-black cast and Jackson enthusiastically agreed.[34] So the faux ancient Egyptian setting, populated with an American comic, sports star, and fashion model might seem a bit corny, but it was a serious and conscious decision to showcase successful African Americans and an ancient culture ruled by blacks in an empowering way.

Even in this setting, Jackson challenges class power through his clothing from the moment we see him: the gold metal plate across his chest is called a gorgerine, worn by the Pharaohs of Egypt as a marker of their regal status.[35] Jackson also sports a formal starched kilt worn by noblemen and officials in ancient Egypt.[36] The other entertainers aren't dressed in this fancy garb. Through his sartorial style, Jackson also plays with time and place, dovetailing past and present through the addition of the gold shirt, black Levis, boots with their leather straps (mimicking the tie-ups on sandals, which everyone else in the film wears), juxtaposing contemporary urban hipness with the ancient Egyptian clothing, creating a hybrid fashion that layers the past, the African past, over the present, but also symbolically transfers the power held by blacks in the past to Jackson, in the present. Leave it to Michael Jackson to reclaim a *regal* African past.

Jackson's hair and make-up also set him apart from everyone else. I can't recall men wearing their hair like this in the early 1990s (except, perhaps, James Brown, although it was never this long). I can recall women

Hollywood stars like Marilyn Monroe wearing their hair like this in the 1950s. The make-up and hair make him look more gender-ambiguous than he had up to this point in his career: glamorous is a word I'd use. There is also a striking difference between the other men in this film, with their well-developed, exposed pecs and biceps, and Jackson's slight and covered frame. His masculinity is distinctly other. And yet *he* is the love interest in the story: we're to believe that the sight of him makes the Queen weak (she swoons before he sings or dances—at the very sight of him) and the point of the lyric is to suggest that they were lovers in the past. What is his allure at this moment? Is it his self-confident (soul man) swagger? His sartorial finery? His difference from the other men? His exoticism, perhaps more convincing here than in "In the Closet"? The kiss between Jackson and Iman is his first on screen, a watershed moment, and it's deep and long (I like that Jackson and Singleton opted to leave in the slight awkwardness, the bumping together of lips, at the beginning of the kiss—there's a hunger to it). He also takes on the conventionally masculine role here, standing over Iman, bending her body backwards as the kiss deepens. (Once again, Jon Pareles found Jackson's "attempt" to look sexy a failure and the romance of this scene unbelievable.)

In contrast to "In the Closet," "Remember the Time" is musically quite simple. The groove is relaxed; except for the opening of "In the Closet" it's the first track that doesn't adhere to the "industrial" sound that so characterizes the album and this makes sense given that it's intended to be nostalgic for a happier, perhaps more innocent time (not only the lover's past, but a different social past). Jackson's vocal for most of the track is warm, creamy, produced in such a way as to emphasize intimacy (through the use of close-miking); before he sings he laughs and says, playfully, "Do you want to try me?" The lush background vocals are equally warm, made more so through the use of extended harmonies; they add considerably to the erotics of the song, not only through the sumptuous harmonies, but also through the long pause on the word "time," which milks those harmonies and does make us long … for something.[37] Like the simple harmonic movement, the song's title is endlessly repeated in both verse and chorus—almost every line of lyric begins with it—an insistent mantra that tries to reconstitute the idyllic past in the present. The place of real intensity and musical change comes during the outro. Jackson's ad libs are forceful, desperate; our aggressive soul man is back. In the short film, the instrumental tracks are removed at this point and Jackson is left to sing by himself, eventually accompanied only by percussion during the choreographed group dance sequence (I've always liked this version better; the intensity of his voice on its own is breathtaking). The dance sequence is there as both an offering to the Queen (the micro-level narrative) and as a celebration of Africa, with its Egyptian-inspired choreography.

Jackson is a trickster in this film, the trickster being a central figure in the folklore of many cultures, including sub-Saharan African, African-American and North American Indigenous cultures. The trickster is a figure who, often using humor as Jackson does here, outwits his powerful adversaries even though he might be physically smaller and hold no power of his own. Henry

Louis Gates describes the original African trickster figure, which he calls Esu, as possessing the qualities of "individuality, satire, parody, irony, magic, indeterminacy, open-endedness, ambiguity, sexuality, chance, uncertainty, disruption and reconciliation, betrayal and loyalty, closure and disclosure, encasement and rupture."[38] Jackson exhibits all these characteristics in the short film, but his appropriation of them exceeds the narrow boundaries of this work. One could characterize Jackson as a trickster *period*, throughout his life and work. While there are many ways in which this idea could be taken up, here I want to focus on Jackson's sexual ambiguity. "The various figures of Esu," Gates writes, "[are] genderless, or of dual gender,"[39] despite the fact that her/his penis figures as significant in many of the stories (and that he/she is often characterized as an "inveterate copulator," which Gates interprets as "the ultimate copula, connecting truth with understanding, the sacred with the profane, text with interpretation," just as Jackson so often does).[40] Gates talks about Esu as "neither male nor female, neither this nor that, but both, a compound morphology."[41] He quotes J. E. and D. M. dos Santos, who say that Esu "inherits all the nature of all the ancestors. He exhibits the characteristics of the male ancestors ... as well as those of the female ... . By compounding their morphology, he partakes indifferently of either group and can circulate freely between them all."[42] "Esu's two sides 'disclose a hidden wholeness;' rather than closing off unity, through the opposition, they signify the passage from one to the other, as sections of a subsumed whole."[43] This describes very well Jackson's easy movement between soul man stud and his soft-spoken self off-stage; between his association and perhaps even identification with female figures such as Diana Ross and Elizabeth Taylor, and his friendships with cool dudes like Chris Tucker; his video-playing friendships with boys and his desire to mother his own and other children. In fact, maybe we're going down the wrong road altogether in trying to talk about Jackson's gender and sexuality through the lenses of white, Western discourse: maybe we need to think not only of tricksters like Esu, but of the traditional ways in which two-spirited people in Indigenous cultures were viewed as "gifted among all beings because they carried two spirits: that of male and female."[44] Jackson himself clearly viewed the boundaries between male and female as too confining. After his death, his make-up artist Karen Faye commented that "he didn't like the line that was drawn between what's allowed for men and what's allowed for women."[45]

*   *   *

There's also a way that Jackson can be linked to the long tradition of dandyism; I know this is not a conventional way to view his performance of gender and I wouldn't in any way place him in the same category as the conventional fop—to the contrary. Dandyism is, first and foremost, linked to the appropriation of class privilege and power by men of lower stature, not necessarily to sexual orientation; as Stan Hawkins writes, it was a "protest against the rule of kings over fashion"[46] and in the case of black dandies, also a protest against racial subjugation. "[D]andifying oneself is about defining oneself as an other"[47] and so it usually involves the use of exaggeration as a means through which to comment on what's being appropriated. To this extent it might also involve the appropriation of traits of femininity as a form of rebellion. This is in part what glam rockers were doing in the 1970s; both Kobena Mercer and Michele Wallace made a comparison between their gender play and Jackson's and noted that while it seemed alright for the likes of Bowie, it was, apparently, "intolerable" for a black man to experiment with gender and sexuality in this way.[48]

In her history of black dandyism, Monica Miller traces the sartorial fight against racial subjugation through the Black Atlantic. Miller writes that from the point of contact between Africa and Europe—before slavery began—the African elite integrated European cloth into their dress, wearing it as a sign of their privilege, but also their otherness: the incorporation of discrete items of European clothing, rather than an entire ensemble, became a marker of authority, since common folk did not have access to it. Miller argues that for African Americans, this "background played a crucial role in determining African American identity … . [I]t is in the mélange of European and African … modes of self-fashioning that black dandyism and dandies in America [and England] developed their aesthetic."[49] Miller gives numerous examples, and one is that of the Pinkster festivals that began in the U.S. in the mid-eighteenth century. The festivals "featured parades and dances of slaves dressed to the nines in clothing normally reserved for their social and racial betters."[50] The participants wore "uniforms, anything but uniform and outfits in which the haphazard dominated as they were matched with an African eye for color."[51] Black Governors and Kings were "elected" on these days; they were men of achievement in the community, respected as elders in a system of slavery designed to limit their humanity and autonomy. One example, Old King Charley, a Pinkster king from the early 1800s, is described as follows: "His costume on this memorable occasion was graphic and unique to the greatest degree, being that work by a British Brigadier of the olden time. Ample broadcloth scarlet coat, with wide flaps almost reaching to his heels, and gaily ornamented everywhere with broad tracings of bright golden lace."[52] To this latter point, Miller notes that with limited access to fine clothes, slaves in the U.S. would often adorn those that they had to make them fancier, sewing on shiny buttons, pieces of lace, or other bits of fine cloth. While there is, of course, a considerable amount of time and history that passes between this tradition and the appearance of Jackson, the practice of African American men "stylin' out" in sartorial finery continued as a means through which to challenge distinctions of race and class. But the Pinkster example resonates with Jackson's style in a particular way.

While the iconic white rhinestone glove, socks, flood pants, and rhinestone jackets had, of course, appeared long prior to *Dangerous*, it was when Jackson hired Michael Bush and Dennis Thompkins to be his dressers in the late 1980s that the markers of Jackson's style really gelled. Indeed, in his book, *Dressing Michael Jackson*, Bush outlines exactly how he and Thompkins—with Jackson's significant input—created the looks that came to be singularly associated with Jackson. A key part of this look was the creation of a silhouette that exaggerated Jackson's relatively slight frame, making him look "taller and broader" to create "the illusion that his physical presence was majestic and grand."[53] This involved using the short jacket to create "hard lines" that pulled horizontally across his chest, ending with shoulder pads, both of which made him look broader. Hard fabrics were used. The jackets were always short to the waist to meet his form-fitting pants. While Bush doesn't comment on the effect of this, the broad chest tapering to the waist in a classic V shape is characteristic of a classically normative male form and signifies physical strength; his "effeminacy," with very few exceptions, did not extend to his dress. The short jacket was taken from British military history and heredity. This piece of information is significant (and I don't think it was widely known until the publication of Bush's book): linking it to Britain specifically connects Jackson's dandyism not only to an American tradition of black stylin' out, but also to the appropriation of British power and privilege. According to Bush, Jackson was fascinated by the history of the British monarchy and its military might. "When we toured in Europe, Michael made it his business to visit castles and ancient cities, where he was mesmerized by museum portraits of kings and queens. He would stare at them along the walls of Buckingham Palace, [the] Tower of London, or the Houses of Parliament, absorbing it all—the glitz, the glamour, the medals and honors, the larger-than-life ways these royals and commanders were portrayed."[54]

Bush makes two other important points about Jackson's style: the first is that it was always intended to be syncretic. One of the things he tried to do was combine the formality and authority of the jacket with something "from the street." The white undershirt was used in this way, as were the black Levi jeans. Jackson wanted the effect of this on those who saw him to be: we're not like you, but yet in some way we are; you are inaccessible, yet accessible; a commoner who has somehow escaped being common (and isn't this true of Jackson).[55] The other important point—and this is the crazy thing we know and perhaps shake our heads at—is Jackson's penchant for excessively adorning those military style jackets. Michael Bush writes that Jackson called this "icing" the coats, or "slinging dust" on them.[56]

Bringing together Bush's narrative with Miller's links Jackson to a long tradition of black dandyism: the appropriation of British military garb, the clothing of white, colonial authority; the hybrid/syncretic style; the adornment of clothing as a principal—adding on to relatively plain clothes to make them fancy, to give the wearer status, to exaggerate the spectacle—these are all age-old techniques of self-styling from Africa and the African diaspora. In a sense, Jackson was like the Pinkster kings and perhaps similarly threatening. As Miller writes: "... for whites and blacks, clothing and fashion were a means by which the status of slave and master, whiteness and blackness, masculinity and femininity, Africanness and Americanness was being determined."[57] Jackson's military style appropriated hyper-masculine privilege and queered it. His entire over-the-top, camp "King of Pop" persona was intended, in the tradition of dandyism, to point not only to a performative appropriation of white, masculine class privilege, but his *real* appropriation of that power through his enormous commercial and artistic success. The fact that he never stepped back from his image—never allowed the public to see him in any other way—in fact, that he continued to exaggerate it as he got older, is what is so unusual and alluring about him. Like a good trickster, we just never knew if he believed himself in the role of King or whether he was putting us on, but in the process he was asking us to think about spectacles of white, masculine privilege.

*   *   *

And then, Jackson made the short film for "In the Closet," which throws out all of his usual dandified trappings. Herb Ritts, known for his black and white, stripped down style of photography, wanted to do away with visual images that had defined Jackson for so long: "It's not about outrageous costumes and 50 dancers this time. It's really about bringing out Michael's energy in a new way."[58] Jackson's otherwise covered body is revealed to the camera as it has not been before, especially risky for him given his vitiligo. He wears a white undershirt—not his usual white undershirt, but a sleeveless tank. This t-shirt signifies the different masculinities of those who've also worn it, such as Freddie Mercury (a look that could be associated with gay men), Bruce Springsteen (working-class cool), Brando in *Streetcar*; the "muscle" shirt or the "wife beater" (a slur to those of lower-class status). Jackson takes on new gendered territory here, but it's not clear what type. He wears black jeans that are *not* too short, that do *not* reveal rhinestone socks, and black boots, not loafers, his hair slicked back into a pony tail, no loose strands, no curls to distract us from his face, which is completely exposed, entirely revealed, lightly made up and often smiling. Could this be the "real" Michael Jackson? Having grown up into this?

Criticisms of this film tend to focus on how much Jackson and Naomi Campbell dance apart and how he doesn't often look at her, but this is erroneous. Consider the details. They dance together as much as they do separately and he makes direct eye contact with her a number of times. In fact, while the Mystery Girl speaks for the third time, Jackson and Campbell stand holding each other, looking into each other's eyes for an extended time; at other moments he sings part of the chorus looking directly at her. There are a lot of "hot" moments in this piece: Jackson's body wave, made in silhouette, that just misses touching Campbell (I think the last time we saw him use this move was in "Beat It"); her tender stroking of his body and the way she shimmies down and back up the length of it, her hands resting on his hips; his gentle caress of her face; and of course the moment of metaphorical penetration, when Jackson dives between Campbell's legs just before the longest, most developed and ecstatic iteration of the chorus begins. It's true that Jackson ends up alone, giving us an incredibly virtuosic solo dance segment at the end of the film, but it's not as though he hasn't interacted with Campbell in a sensual and sexual way throughout the film. And it seems, perhaps too oddly for some to contemplate, that he knows his way around a woman. Failure? I don't think so. Threatening? Probably.

Utopia

"Black dreams are not about utopia—how could they be?"
Elizabeth Chin

Jackson often said that he wanted to offer people some "escape" or "release" through his art. His autobiography, *Moonwalk*, ends with these words: "To me, nothing is more important than making people happy, giving them a release from their problems and worries, helping to lighten their load."[1] Even in what, I suppose, are his final public words, spoken towards the end of the film *This Is It*, he repeated this sentiment. "It's a great adventure," he tells his musicians, dancers, and crew. "There's nothing to be nervous about. They just want wonderful experiences, they want escapism, we wanna take them places they've never been before, we wanna show them talent they've never seen before. So give your all." This way of framing his art drove rock critic Dave Marsh, and probably others who didn't express it quite so vehemently, absolutely crazy: over and over again in his 1985 book, Marsh slammed Jackson for describing his art as "escapism," interpreting the description as facile, a sign that Jackson viewed what he did as fluffy entertainment, easily forgotten commodified pap, rather than serious art. For those, especially those on the left, who are committed to thinking deeply about the world and its problems, the notion of escape is anathema to a politics of change. Art that is "political" should move us more deeply *into* an issue; it should challenge our thinking, be difficult, make us squirm. Critics with their "well-worn war chest of poststructuralism pieties"[2] which are dominated by negative critique, skepticism and a "hermeneutics of suspicion" (as philosopher Paul Ricoeur called it) are wary of the idea of escape as holding any kind of radical potential. Escape suggests that we'd rather not think too much, that we're turning our back on, rather than facing up to problems. It sometimes also gets linked to the Marxist idea that "escape" in the form of leisure, is necessary for the smooth running of capitalism—some small release valve so that things don't overheat and eventually explode, but nothing that will in any way challenge the system; leisure in this paradigm is also tied to consumption, to music as commodity and despite a lot of writing on popular music (mine included) that argues for the possibility of commodified music such as Jackson's to serve as a means through which our subjectivities can be formed, our ideas about social life broadened or changed, the concept that this is just false consciousness persists. Still, Jackson's idea echoes what film studies scholar Richard Dyer writes about the idea of escape as it is linked to entertainment in general: "Entertainment offers the image of 'something better' to escape into, or something we want deeply that our day to day lives don't provide."[3] Jackson, by the way, also often called what he did "entertainment," another way in which he was seen to diminish his art. Dyer links this idea of entertainment as escape to utopianism: "[a]lternatives, hopes, wishes—these are the stuff of utopia, the sense that things could be better."[4] He argues that this "responds to a real need created by [the failings and inadequacies of] society."[5] And he makes the important point that so much commercial entertainment is made by those who are on the margins of society—by racial and sexual minorities who through their art have a hand in shaping the utopic impulse in entertainment. Might Jackson have expanded on the idea of his art as "escapism," possibly even taking up some of the issues I've just raised? Yes. But like many artists, he mostly preferred to let his work speak for itself; his effort went into producing, not commenting upon it. It's pretty clear that he considered commentary and explanation to lessen the effect, to demystify, to detract from the possibility of escaping. (Relevant aside: when the patent for Jackson's "Smooth Criminal" "lean" shoes was made public, revealing how he had been able seemingly to defy gravity on stage, he said to his costumer Michael Bush "I just want to know why, Bush … . It was supposed to stay magical. Why would they ruin it for everybody?"[6]) Certainly this must have been the reason why, in a note he penned to himself in 1979, only recently made public, he wrote, "*I will do no interviews. I will be magic.*"[7] Mission accomplished.

As Dyer makes clear, escape is a pretty important function of art. At its most basic, it suggests that there is a way to be temporarily transported out of a here and now that might range from boring to debilitating—it might offer a moment of relief. And we need moments of relief. Such moments are not about abdicating responsibility (well, some of them might be and that's okay too), but about creating in both body and mind the space to imagine different or *possible* worlds. Escaping might mean *feeling* a different way, changing your body chemistry, momentarily stepping into love, euphoria, bliss, empathy, a strong sense of community—or anger, fear, hurt. It's no great revelation to say that many people use art, and certainly music, for this purpose all the time, but it's not generally viewed as very revolutionary, especially when the music under discussion is "mainstream" pop.

There's recently been, however, a resurgence of interest in thinking about performance in terms that link the idea of "escapism," in the more capacious sense I've used it above, to the utopian. Jill Dolan and José Muñoz both write about the utopian in performance as a means through which to reanimate a discourse of hope, going against the grain of what Muñoz describes as a "[critical] climate ... [which] is dominated by a dismissal of political idealism." "Shouting down utopia is an easy move ... [it] has always been vulnerable to charges of naïveté, impracticality, or lack of rigor."[8] We're not talking, necessarily, about performances that offer *representations* of utopia, of some neat idea of a future world; Dolan's argument in particular is that you can experience a utopian moment during a performance that may have absolutely nothing to do with utopia per se. She writes about glimpsing it through what she calls "utopian performatives:"[9]

> small but profound moments in which performance calls the attention of the audience in a way that lifts everyone slightly above the present, into a hopeful feeling of

what the world might be like if every moment of our lives were as emotionally voluminous, generous, aesthetically striking, and intersubjectively intense … . Utopian performatives, in their doings, make palpable an affective vision of how the world might be better.

Utopian performatives can be gleaned in, for example, three steps of a moonwalk (wasn't that moment at the *Motown 25* celebration utopian?), made possible through Jackson's incomparable skill as a performer, his love of the fantastic, of larger-than-life spectacle, as well as his refusal ever to step out of character, on or off stage, so that the utopian impulse we might feel during his performances is carried into his, and by extension our, everyday lives. Jackson was interested in creating utopian performatives through astonishment, which Ernst Bloch considered "an important philosophical mode of contemplation … . Astonishment helps one surpass the limitations of an alienating present-ness and allows one to see a different time and place."[10] I've experienced such astonishment many, many times while listening to and watching Michael Jackson, both on and off stage, from the jaw-dropping way every nuance of the ballad "Human Nature" was channeled through his dancing body in live performance, to the mind-blowing precision and complexity of the group dancing in live performances of "Dangerous." Steven Shaviro captures the power and beauty of Jackson's utopian performatives (what he calls, after Bloch and Frederic Jameson the "utopian dimension"), by calling attention to "the modulations of Michael's voice, the sinuous movements of his dancing, the way that his musical arrangements took disco and r&b and gave them both a smoothness and a slightly alien sheen ... allowed to blossom into a new aestheticized state in which pop crassness had itself become a rare, almost Wildean, delicacy.[11]

*   *   *

I'm making the assumption that you're listening to *Dangerous* from start to finish as you read, a listening practice that's become more or less obsolete, but one that was not, yet, when the album was released. So when you've come through the first six songs, battered and bruised (in a good way) by the force of those grooves, that noise, the angst, suspiciousness, intense sexual energy of Jackson's voice, and the worldly complications espoused in the lyrics, there are two likely responses to the opening keyboard strains of "Heal the World:" relief or disbelief. Juxtaposed with what has come before it—a relatively unified, black, sound world that's been sustained now for better than half an hour of listening—the saccharine strains of "Heal the World" seem out of place, if not completely out of character. Jackson obviously wanted extreme contrast, he wanted to shift abruptly into another world. Of course he was always capable of moving among musical genres, or blending them together—his crossover success was dependent upon such skillful manipulations. But such an abrupt turn to a mainstream (white) ballad form with vastly different production values was unheard of on his previous albums. Moreover, on his earlier records the ballads are conventional love songs—somehow it's less corny to sing sweetly about love than it is about world peace—and his most self-reflexive song about changing himself as a means through which to change the world was generically tied to gospel ("Man in the Mirror"): no credibility gap there. But how do you hold the same audience for "Heal the World" as for what came before it on this album? How do you reconcile the hip sounds of "Jam" with the sentimental sweetness of "Heal the World"? While there is so much that is cutting edge and "contemporary" sounding about the first six songs on *Dangerous*, "Heal the World" is full of the conventions and clichés that can be, and were, easily dismissed. On top of that, the song was thought by some critics, like *Rolling Stone*'s Alan Light, to be "a hallmark-card knockoff of 'We Are the World.'" It's not only formulaic in and of itself, then, but it's perceived as trying to repeat—and crassly capitalize upon?—a formula that was used to raise money for hungry kids in Africa.

Here's the thing, though. "Heal the World" is not much like "We Are the World" except that they both might be considered anthemic. "We Are the World" is a soulful ballad that draws heavily on gospel and blues conventions and singing that digs deep into the well of empathy. Soul has gone AWOL on "Heal the World." And Jackson was too prolific, virtuosic, meticulous, and self-conscious an artist to offer this seemingly fluffy idea without good reason. By all accounts he wrote and recorded hundreds of tracks for every album and made sure that only the strongest made the final cut (I suppose naysayers could argue that he sometimes had bad taste). And maybe "Heal the World" is too sentimental a ballad for some, but Jackson claimed in an internet chat with his fans in 2001 that if he could only perform one of his songs for the rest of his life, this would be it.[12] And the trouble is, it doesn't sound like an ironic statement. Really, out of all his astonishingly good music, this takes pride of place? My take is that "Heal the World" serves as an important thematic pivot point on *Dangerous*, moving the listener from the worldly, noisy complications of the opening tracks into a somewhat troubling vision of utopia. He does, indeed, want to escape what has come before with this song, into the comfort of convention, into stillness, and as has been noted by others, he wanted to make it simple so that people could sing along.[13] I pair this song with "Black or White" because it, too, is in part about envisioning a better world, although musically, lyrically and in the short film, cracks and fissures that remain somewhat hidden in "Heal the World" reappear there with a vengeance. Fascinating that Jackson placed these utopic songs at the very center of the record, a structural decision that gives them considerable weight; fascinating that he felt it necessary to offer *two* utopic visions, one so general, the other specifically about race, and that they are placed back to back. And fascinating that this is the moment when children's voices are heard for the first time on a Jackson record, in both songs.

In fact, let me just rest on this point for a moment, because it's so extraordinary: Jackson's two utopic songs both feature children's voices prominently. On one level, I believe that "Heal the World" and "Black or White" were both written primarily *for* children—and to permit adults to feel as and with children—as well as putting children squarely at the center of two weighty issues Jackson takes up on this record: racial equality and the search for unity and healing. Joseph Vogel agrees that certainly in "Black or White," "the decision to appeal to children was both deliberate and strategic on Jackson's part. He believed children were the audience most likely to be open and receptive to his message—and most likely to facilitate the social changes he relays in the song and film."[14] *Dangerous* is the first Jackson record to feature children's voices, but it isn't the last. They appear on both *HIStory* and *Invincible*, when the song calls out for healing or represents healing: in one of the most poignant examples, a child calls out to him by name during the instrumental interlude of "Stranger in Moscow;" and "They Don't Care About Us" begins with children chanting, defiantly. Both these songs are direct responses to the 1993 allegations of child abuse; it's particularly poignant to me that in the face of that accusation, Jackson would, in his beautiful but gut-wrenchingly sad response, "Stranger in Moscow," see not only a child but a "beggar boy" as the one to lift him out of his grief. Tavia Nyong'o makes a similar point about the *HIStory* teaser film, when he notes that the only person to speak is a little boy who cries out "Michael, I love you," a choice that "seemed to echo unwisely the speculations and accusations that dogged the superstar."[15] Jackson clearly did not care about misguided perceptions.

Finding a place for children on an album otherwise occupied by adult concerns is a bold move, perhaps one of the most "adult" things Jackson does on this record and one that perhaps only he, with his multi-generational appeal, could have pulled off: imagine children appearing in the middle of *Achtung Baby*, *Nevermind*, or *It Takes a Nation of Millions to Hold us Back*! Right. This move actually opens the album up to address concerns other than Jackson's own struggles with the world, in voices other than his (challenging the perception that everything MJ did was about MJ). On "Heal the World," his voice *gives way* to a child's at the end of the song and "Black or White" opens with the defiant voice of child actor Macaulay Culkin. These frames work to decenter/ destabilize not only adults in general, but Jackson himself from the songs' messages; his image is also completely absent from the short film for "Heal the World." Within the context of the album, "Heal the World" offers a moment of respite, something we don't ever get on albums like *Achtung Baby* or *Nevermind*. Reveling in me, my problems, my world, my angst is a young man's game, it's the spirit of youthful rebelliousness on which rock 'n' roll was built. Jackson's take on the world is much more capacious, and actually includes a place both for kids and hope. As Armond White has written, "[Jackson's] after something purer and better than the childish, rockist idea of pop as rebellion. Jackson knows culture is more than that."[16]

What Jackson does not do in introducing children into his utopic visions, importantly, is buy into conventional ideas of normative futurity, i.e. that the future belongs to children, or: what we can't achieve ourselves, our children will achieve on our behalf. In the collection of short films that accompanies *Dangerous*, Jackson says in a preamble to "Heal the World:" "Being with [children] connects us to the deep wisdom of life, the simple goodness shines straight from their hearts." Many conventional ideas about childhood link it to the future through the belief that children enter the world as empty vessels, that there is, therefore, an opportunity—or obligation—to educate them, "fill" them, shape them, in order that they will hopefully produce a "better" future (this is tied to a narrative of progress that has been much critiqued in the wake of poststructuralism), that they will fulfill the dreams of their parents, and that they will carry on family lines.[17] But Jackson rarely talks or sings about children in this conventional way (the lines in "Heal the World" are about making it better for *you, me, the entire human race* and children). For him, there was a utopian impulse in children not because they represent the future, the hopes and dreams of adults, the continuation of a "normal" progression of time and family, but because their honesty, simplicity and innocence center adults, bring us back to feeling, to good affect; "now, when the world is so confused and its problems so complicated," he says in the same preamble, "we need our children more than ever." Elsewhere he wrote: "In their innocence, very young children know themselves to be light and love. If we allow them, they can teach us to see ourselves the same way."[18]

In fact Jackson's thoughts about children as grounding adults and his own predilection to hang out with them and enjoy what he calls in the song "Childhood" "elementary things" corresponds to Judith Halberstam's discussion about "queering time and space." Halberstam notes that "in Western cultures, we chart the emergence of the adult from the dangerous and unruly period of adolescence as a desired process of maturation; and we create longevity as the most desirable future ... and pathologize modes of living that show little or no concern for [these]." Marriage, reproduction, the "normal scheduling of daily life," passing values and goods from generation to generation "connect the family to the future of both familial and national stability."[19] When these normal ideas of the occupation of time and space are challenged through a life that is differently lived, there is a lot at stake; Halberstam notes that it is "a way of life" that is disrupted and this makes people, like Jackson, who travelled a different path, pretty threatening.

*   *   *

One of the reasons—perhaps the main one—that "Heal the World" is so easy to write off is because it's so laden with convention. There's a deep-rooted suspicion of convention in Western culture. It makes us worry about big issues like individuality, originality, progress— modernist ideas, to be sure, but certainly still with us however much we might think we've moved beyond them. We think that conventions make for meaningless art, or art so over-determined that it can't be very significant; kind of like we're tapping into someone else's head, like we can't even come up with an idea that's our own. But as musicologist Susan McClary wrote so eloquently in her book *Conventional Wisdom*, "... a great deal of wisdom resides in conventions: nothing less than the premises of an age, the cultural arrangements that enable communication, co-existence and self-awareness ... . [I]t is not the deviations alone that signify, but the norms as well."[20] So what are the conventions used in "Heal the World," and how do they work, socially?

The chords played at the opening of this song make it seem as if time has momentarily stood still. We're pausing for reflection, getting away from the rigid and hectic conception of time established in the (long) opening sequence of songs. Time is more elastic here (through the use of rubato), and the sounds are prettier: warm, rich chords gently rocking back and forth between tension and resolution, like being rocked in a musical cradle. The keyboard is dominant—an instrument, as I noted in the previous chapter, historically considered softer, more "feminine." Industrial noise is replaced by the sound of children's voices; a little girl offers the opening spoken message. After this introduction, when the groove begins, the melody climbs upward, as does the movement in the bass, a classic device for suggesting optimism in Western music (metaphorically rising up out of the depths). The song is set in a major key, historically associated with happiness, with only a brief turn to the minor mode—predictably during the moment when Jackson questions "then why do we keep straying … ." Phrases are absolutely regular and simply constructed: the music is repeated for the first four lines of lyric in each verse and Jackson, uncharacteristically, does not tamper with the melody; he sings it absolutely straight and the same every time.

There's another convention that Jackson uses in this song that he absolutely loved: modulation, or key change, up by a step. When the chorus is repeated about four and a half minutes into the song, you suddenly feel as though you've been lifted a little higher and then it happens again, at about five minutes. It's one of those musical conventions that gets a bad rap because it's so dramatic, intended to up the emotional impact with a bang—and in Western culture, emotional bangs are frowned upon (it's a class thing; being sophisticated requires showing some restraint, being less obvious). Sudden modulations happen frequently in pop music of a certain kind, the sentimental kind, and usually towards the end of a song—think Celine's "My Heart Will Go On," or Whitney's "I Will Always Love You," or Bon Jovi's "Livin' on a Prayer."

The choir comes in at the first modulation—conventional—and something profound happens here. Jackson almost absents himself completely from this uplifting moment. It's not unusual for this to serve as the point in a song when the singer stops singing the melody and starts to improvise, as Jackson does in "Man in the Mirror." This allows for the emotional intensity of the song to grow. But in "Heal the World," Jackson is curiously restrained at this point as he is throughout the song. There is little tension in his voice; his dramatic use of vibrato is used sparingly; he never rises above a soft-to-medium volume level. Even when he reaches into his beautiful falsetto, he seems to exert no more energy than elsewhere. I can't think of another instance in Jackson's output where he so holds back.

It's significant that in his central utopian song on *Dangerous*, he recedes to the background, letting children and the chorus (the community) present the vision. Why? Think about the details that I've elaborated and put them together with the song's genre: it's a ballad that belongs to the white mainstream of pop music. It's one of the whitest-sounding songs Jackson ever made. He was certainly capable of taking white forms and making them sound blacker, but he doesn't do that here. The conventions that I've talked about all point in the direction of musical whiteness: the key (this isn't a modal piece), the regularity—even musical squareness—the near absence of improvisation or call and response; there isn't a blue note to be found. The timbre of Jackson's voice. His uncharacteristically bland emotional palette also points to a particular idea of restraint and respectability in mainstream white pop music, a reflection of the desirability of these characteristics in middle class white culture. Indeed, even the little girl speaking at the beginning of the song sounds white.

It's entirely possible that Jackson just wanted complete rest at this point on the album (but interesting how even that idea can get conflated, musically, with whiteness: restful, "respectable" bodies); and we could stick with the idea that it's so simple because he wanted it to be anthemic and easy for others to sing. Receding into the background of the song could be said to demonstrate the idea that unity and healing require selflessness: let the choir take the utopian moment by themselves; let the child's voice take over near the end of the song. In fact, let Michael become the child, let his voice melt into that of the child's, let him become as the child—another of his many physical transformations and perhaps the one he would have liked best. This too symbolically removes the idea of the child from futurity and strengthens the idea that adults *become* as children (as Christ suggested) to "solve the world's problems." We could understand this song in those terms, at "face value," and it would still be revolutionary, wouldn't it? It would still be a bold statement to make in the middle of a gritty and musically complex record.

But I can't shake the connection to whiteness, especially as I read this song up against some very insightful analyses of "Black or White." "Black or White," in fact, is Jackson's most deeply scrutinized song. There isn't another of his works that has generated as much, or as insightful commentary and that is, perhaps, because the short film that accompanied the song represents a watershed political moment in his artistic output, as well as having generated the most serious backlash against Jackson to that point.

*   *   *

"Black or White" was the first single released from *Dangerous* and with it, Jackson clearly intended to set the tone of this record as being more overtly political than any of his previous offerings. Both the song and the short film are complex, nuanced examples of what Henry Louis Gates calls "signifyin(g)," the revisioning of previous works or styles, especially those belonging to the dominant culture, through the lens of difference.[21] So, for example, the main riff of the song, as David Brackett notes, is taken from the Stones' "Soul Survivor," a song off one of the most classic of white rock albums, *Exile on Main Street*.[22] It's a bold move of re-appropriation, since the Stones were heavily indebted to black music. In contrast, one of the two middle sections of "Black or White" belongs to rap. What's perhaps less often noticed is that the bass line is indebted to funk, not rock; that the music played underneath the opening dialogue is MOR rock, and that the middle section borrows stylistically from metal. Jackson obviously juxtaposes these musical styles to drive home the utopic theme of racial unity: difference can co-exist harmoniously. As Brackett points out, however, juxtaposing different musical styles in this obvious way has the effect of *pointing to* their differences, rather than obscuring them; we probably notice the stylistic distinctions more forcefully in "Black or White" because they are side by side or layered over each other, whereas in a more generically "pure" song, or in a song where genres are more seamlessly blended together, we're less likely to have our attention drawn to the issue of genre and its cultural connotations. And Jackson complicates the generic juxtapositions. There are two middle-eight sections in this piece: the first is Jackson's diatribe against racial inequality ("I am tired of this devil"), which employs the language of metal, the second is the rap section, written and performed by Jackson's white producer, Bill Bottrell. As Lisha McDuff has pointed out, metal, a genre characteristically associated with white men, is here appropriated by the black artist as a means through which to express rage at racial injustice (that's already complicated); "feel good" rap is appropriated by the white artist, "deliberately confusing musical codes."[23] In a more conventional rendering of musical genre, Jackson might have invited a black rapper to express the sentiments of the "sheets" section. But Jackson often used rock music to express anger, especially in his later works: it became one of his go to genres for this purpose and it makes sense that he would draw on a musical style rooted in rebellion.[24] The rap section sounds "inauthentic," too white and, in the context of late 1980s and early 1990s politically and musically heavy rap music, like a nod to the likes of Vanilla Ice. Bottrell's version was meant by him to be a demo—as he said, he "didn't think much of white rap"— with the intent that a "real" rapper would cut the final version, but Jackson insisted on keeping it.[25] Why? After all, he used black rappers elsewhere on this record; why on the song most overtly about race and race relations would he hand over the genre most associated with expressing racial inequities at this historical moment to, in effect, the oppressor (not Bottrell himself, of course, but to whiteness as we hear it through his voice) and turn, himself, to a white genre in order to express his rage about racial hatred?

These are beautiful examples of the practice of signifyin(g). Jackson liked the idea of upsetting the generic apple cart, especially within the context of this song, which is so explicitly about race. But upsetting it how, exactly? Do we take it at face value—either the simple, and oft-noted juxtaposition of genres as a metaphor for racial equality, or the generic reversal (whites doing rap; blacks doing metal), both of which suggest, on the surface, racial utopia? Or do we read it— and by "it," I now mean genre as it operates in the entire song—as a musical statement that creates a white utopic vision of racial equality?

*   *   *

Perhaps it's time to bring the short film for "Black or White" into the mix. The film premiered on network television in November, 1991 to a world-wide audience estimated at around five hundred million people. A great number of them were shocked by what they saw, even though in the larger context of violence and sexuality in pop culture it was pretty tame. The film begins with the camera taking the viewer on a ride, down out of the

clouds and through the streets of a suburban neighborhood (like a video game) finally resting on a single
house, where white Dad watches a baseball game on TV,
while white Mom reads the tabloid press. Upstairs, in
the sanctity of his bedroom, their young son imagines
himself as a rock star, playing air guitar while jumping
on his bed. It's interesting that Jackson chose notable
actors to play the male roles (George Wendt of *Cheers*;
Macaulay Culkin of *Home Alone*), while Mom is a much
less well-known actress (Tess Harper): I understand
Mom as a blank and generic suburban housewife. Jackson
wanted the focus to be on power dynamics within white
patriarchy and Mom's disempowered and non-celebrity
status is part of that.

Dad becomes irritated and demands that the child
turn the music down—it's too late and too loud, and the
music is garbage: the kid is wasting his time. The socially-
important message of the song that follows, and which
Dad is forced to reckon with as he is catapulted out of his
house by his child's deafening guitar power chord, clearly
proves that he is wrong about this music: *very* wrong. He
is, in fact, hurled back to Africa, armchair and all, and
watches Jackson dance with African tribesmen (Jackson
plays air guitar here, too, just like Culkin—is this meant
to suggest that Culkin has *become* Jackson, that Jackson is
reappropriating rock from whiteness, or that the music
Culkin was rocking out to is, ultimately, derived from the
blues?). The short film for "Remember the Time" came
after this, but it, too, invoked Africa; the invocations were
clearly part of Jackson's new racial politics, a politics
that included recalling and celebrating origins. Like
the generic juxtapositions of the music, the vignettes of

Jackson dancing with different ethnic groups point our attention to cultural difference and position Jackson as the one to bridge it. At the same time, the vignettes are exposed as constructions, as taking place on a Hollywood soundstage. As Joseph Vogel notes, "It is almost as if Jackson is simultaneously celebrating cosmopolitanism, while exposing the superficial displays that often fall under its guise."[26] Vogel also makes the important point that these vignettes are not only about *racial* harmony: "Jackson features vibrant women of all colors and nationalities with whom he dances reciprocally .... Jackson is, in a sense, representative of the 'new man' replacing the white patriarch."[27] It's crucial to note this because critics often viewed Jackson as misogynistic and fearful of women, but he engaged with them in his work in a multitude of different ways. In fact, Willa Stillwater's analysis of "Smooth Criminal" convincingly reads it as a response to the misogyny of the "Girl Hunt Ballet" in the film *The Bandwagon*, itself based on detective fiction of the Mickey Spillane variety, where women are killed senselessly and as a matter of course. Where these stories dispose of women as points in a plot, Jackson stops to consider the woman who is the victim of these crimes ("Annie, are you okay?").[28]

The vignettes in "Black or White" are interrupted by the "sheets" section, during which Jackson walks aggressively towards the camera through raging flames that obscure images of a burning cross and war. Following this, and mirroring the opening of the film, the camera zooms in on Jackson and a small posse of kids on the steps of urban row houses—little Macaulay has been transplanted from his suburban tedium to urban hipness, trading in rock for rap in the process and he lip-synchs the rap, once again miming a musical style (copying rather than creating: an encapsulation of the history of white/black musical relations). Jackson emerges from the scene perched atop the Statue of Liberty, the "iconic, torch-bearing 'Mother of Exiles,' and symbol of melting-pot possibility," yet the first line he sings from this perch mocks the whole idea: "Don't tell me you agree with me / When I saw you kicking dirt in my eye."[29] As the camera pulls back, the Statue becomes one of many architectural symbols of nationhood, past and present (Big Ben, The Acropolis, the Egyptian pyramids, the Taj Mahal, the Eiffel Tower), representing the idea of global unity while retaining individual difference. The famous face-morphing scene follows and that quickly came to serve as the final act in the film. But in the original version, of course, it was followed by Jackson's "panther dance" and it was this that made all hell break loose for him and which also allowed us to see what he was really up to in the first part of the short film.

As Eric Lott has written, "something so extraordinary happened at this moment that the video's initial audiences couldn't take it in."[30] The camera pulls back from the morphing scene to expose a film set and crew, the last (black) actress to appear in the morphing scene and the film's director, John Landis, yelling "cut" and saying to the actress "that was perfect; how do you do that?" There's no answer to this question: how could there be? For the question is only superficially about a feat of modern technology; a white man has just asked a black woman how she manages to adapt as a minority, in which she must move both as part of her own world and that of the dominant culture and be cheerful in the process ("that was perfect [behavior]"), a world of double-consciousness. Lott and, more recently, Elizabeth Chin view the moment at which the film set is revealed as that which exposes the depictions of ethnic minorities and the cheery vision of racial unity earlier in the film as a construction, a fabrication of the white, Hollywood imagination. The fact that these images are framed by whiteness—Culkin's suburban family at the opening and Simpson's at the end—strongly suggests, as Chin points out, that this is a narrative largely about white perceptions. Indeed, the earlier vignettes have already implied that race is a social construction, and pointed to the monodimensional ways in which it is constructed in the white imagination, although we have to be careful about pushing this idea too far. In the midst of what we might too easily wish to characterize as "stereotypes," there are also "realistic" (I'm shying away from the word "authentic") depictions of ethnic dances, such as the Jingle Dress Dance, performed by the little Indigenous girl; it's especially jarring that this takes place against one of the most stereotypical Hollywood images of American Indians: the horse-back riding, hollering guys from classic Westerns.[31] Still, the elaborate set that is revealed at the end of the morphing scene suggests, as Chin notes, the concentrated effort it requires to build and maintain Hollywood fantasies. Jackson's "panther dance" makes this interpretation all the more clear.

As the camera pulls back, not only is the Hollywood set left behind, but so is the director. Joe Vogel calls the panther dance a "coup d'etat of the camera ... the white director has been symbolically dethroned" (and apparently John Landis was literally abandoned as director at this point, actively discouraging much of what Jackson wanted to do, Jackson himself taking over as "auteur").[32] A black panther appears and slinks into an alley way—not a brightly lit street, filled with middle class folks, as in Gene Kelly's *Singing in the Rain*, from which Jackson appropriates. The panther—an obvious allusion to the Black Panther Party—morphs into Jackson, who embarks on a truly extraordinary four minute solo dance. Chin views this dance as belonging to the genre of the black dream ballet in Hollywood film, pioneered by the dancer Katherine Dunham in the film *Stormy Weather*.[33] Chin's argument is that black performers often "refrain entirely from exploring their own versions of escape and wish fulfillment, versions that are likely to be at odds with those imposed by dominant society."[34] They entertain for the pleasure of white audiences, setting aside their own dreams, tempering their artistry, or shaping it to please the audience. One of the functions of the black dream ballet is to offer the black artist a space in which s/he can express and dream on their own terms. The "panther dance" is such a moment for Jackson.

There is no music *per se* during the panther dance: the song proper has ended on a big, fat concluding cadence. Armond White's reading is that "[t]here's no [conventional] music because Jackson, who's been performing since childhood, has no tradition for the musical expression of anger,"[35] and although this is an interesting idea, it forgets the "sheets" section of the song, where Jackson uses the language of metal to express a good deal of anger. There *is* sound during the panther dance, sound that harkens back to the noisy beginnings of the record. Lisha McDuff views it as a "complex layering of sound that feels more like an avant-garde composition, exploring the musical value of all kinds of [non-musical sounds] … . It's possible that this alternative musical expression is another form of protest as well."[36] Indeed. Here we understand just how central an idea noise as protest is to this album. That breaking glass heard at the beginning of the record—that very first sound—can now truly be understood as the sound not only of a broken world, but as anger about part of what's broken—anger about racial prejudice. Jackson "brings the noise" to this problem with as much force as hip hop did, although apparently with too much ambiguity for a lot of folks to understand it.

Jackson begins his dance trepidatiously. After he emerges from the form of the panther he stands still for a moment, settling into his new skin, unsure how to move forward. He dons his fedora and is caught in a spotlight, invoking the idea of the panopticon, which Michel Foucault used as a metaphor for the pervasive surveillance and disciplining (normalizing) of bodies in contemporary society.[37] A close-up captures Jackson's bowed head, which he slowly raises so that his eyes meet the camera. While there is so much that is extraordinary about the dance that follows, this moment is perhaps one of the richest in the film. His performances, both live and on film, were just about the only time we ever saw Jackson's eyes, since he covered them with sunglasses when he was off stage. But even to have the camera rest on a close-up of his face for as long as it does here is unusual. His gaze is direct, piercing, unwavering, and knowing. He returns the panopticon's disciplining gaze and reverses it; he's watching the watchers, he will not be disciplined, he will appropriate from them, as he demonstrates in the exquisite dance, full of re-readings of Gene Kelly in "Singing In the Rain," and Fred Astaire in "Limehouse Blues" from *Ziegfield Follies*,[38] turning these narratives of white privilege dark. He makes direct reference to Spike Lee's "Do the Right Thing," throwing a trash can through the storefront, defacing white property. After dancing and striking a few beautiful tableaus with his body, he extends the metaphor of the reversed panopticon by walking out into the alley—into public space, space that he *claims*. He braces himself against a storm. When it passes, the shot of his face looking into the camera is repeated. The surveilled is surveilling.

*   *   *

Amidst a sea of complaints from viewers and television executives, Jackson immediately released a statement after the premiere of "Black or White" saying that it upset him to think the film might incite someone to violent or sexually aggressive behavior, and the "panther dance" was either cut completely or shown with racial epithets scrawled as graffiti on the car windows and building facades, carefully positioned so they would seem to be the direct targets of Jackson's rage. Elizabeth Chin talks about the addition of the graffiti as an "act of violence" made "in the interest of protecting white sensibilities."[39] The addition of the graffiti is also an affront to that art form—as if graffiti art is largely about badly-scribbled racial slurs. And the complete excision of the "panther dance" constituted another violence, against Jackson as an artist, in the interest of protecting white sensibilities. The dance is one of the most powerful, technically exquisite performances he ever gave; it was his utopian performative, which got ripped out of his repertory—it's still difficult to find the original version of this short film. Why did he capitulate? Was he afraid of losing his audience? Did he really, in the end, have so little power within the industry? Or could it be that he knew, full well, that the outrage, misunderstanding, and his submission worked perfectly to drive home the point that people were not ready to confront structural racism. To that end, he made the right move.

Soul

My goal in life is to give to the world what I was lucky to receive: the ecstasy of divine union through my music and my dance. It's like my purpose, it's what I'm here for. Michael Jackson

In northern European art of the fifteenth century, the polyptych was a multi-panel painting that commonly served as an altarpiece in a church or cathedral; the form was considered a high point in Christian art. Among the most famous are the Ghent Altarpiece by Hubert and Jan Van Ecyk, *The Last Judgment* by Hans Memling, the *Madonna della Misericordia* by Piera della Francesca and Hieronymous Bosch's *Garden of Earthly Delights*. Mark Ryden's painting for the album cover of *Dangerous*—created with Jackson's input[1]—borrows from this tradition of sacred art. The painting is a triptych, with three "panels" that in the fifteenth century would have been made from wood and hinged together. Normally, the triptych depicts a saint or Christ in the center panel, the side panels comprised of saints associated with the central figure. One can see this "triumvirate" arrangement in Ryden's painting (with the obvious associations): Jackson, central, is flanked by the Dog King, inspired by the 1806 painting of Napoleon by Auguste Dominique Ingres,[2] and the Bird Queen, modeled on a similar figure in Bosch. Many other elements are influenced by the Bosch, which doesn't include such a triumvirate. It's meant to be read left to right, beginning in paradise, and ending in hell, with a mass of humanity in various states of suffering. Ryden's vision isn't as straightforward; the suffering people, body parts, and skeletons that are neatly separated into Bosch's "hell" scenario are dispersed throughout Ryden's painting. Dismemberment is not considered part of suffering (Jackson's stone hand—so identifiable because of its taped fingers—lovingly supports a child, while in Bosch, the dismembered hand has a knife stuck through it); nor is death itself, if we're to believe the grimacing skull held by the child and the skeletal remains of extinct animals enjoying the frivolity of a carnival ride.

That's because the other artistic tradition informing this painting is surrealism. Born out of witnessing "the shock of the traumatized psyche" of World War I, surrealists created art that played on the "[dream-like] disorientation witnessed by" leaders of the movement such as André Breton.[3] For Breton, surrealism aimed for artistic expression in which "life and death, the real and the imagined, the past and the future, the communicable and incommunicable, the heights and the depths cease to be perceived as contradictory."[4] This is precisely what Ryden captures in his painting. He collapses categories in the figures that are represented: living, dead, immortal (cherubs); human, non-human and extinct animals; young, old, historical, present, future, Jackson (now and then, in the *Thriller* years, as a child), fictional, non-fictional, the blending of animate and inanimate objects (the hands that belong to the thrones at the top of the image); partial (Jackson's hand, the skull); hybrid (the Dog King's foot is human). The gender of the child holding the skull is ambiguous: is it a little boy or girl? All this blurring takes place in the completely symmetrical structure of the triptych, a structure that invites us back into binaries and allows us to make some sense of the chaos: male and female (the Dog King and Bird Queen), happy and sad (the clowns perched on either side of Jackson's eyes; there are also happy and sad monkey images on either side of the painting); entering the carnival ride under the sign of the Jolly Roger and exiting under the sign of the all-seeing eye. This last "binary" is a tricky one: could it be that these symbols are meant, respectively, to represent the profane and sacred? The eye image appears in many other places in Jackson's work—in the *HIStory* "teaser" film, and the *Invincible* album artwork.[5] The emphasis on Jackson's own eyes on the *Dangerous* cover links him to this sacred symbol. It does look as though one might enter that ride in one form and exit as another: a skeleton, the child Michael, a Michael Jackson fan; whether this is desirable or downright scary is a matter of interpretation.

The rich imagery in this painting can certainly be read in many ways. It's the most complex of Jackson's album covers and among the most complex in pop music history, more in line with album art in the "serious" rock, rather than pop tradition. One wonders whether it's meant to signify on The Beatles' *Sgt. Pepper's* album cover, with its multitude of characters and multiple images of The Beatles themselves. There is the allusion to the circus—P. T. Barnum appears front and center, with Tom Thumb perched on his head—perhaps as a nod to Jackson's public circus-like image, but also to the well-known story that Jackson considered Barnum's ideas about creating "the greatest show on earth" the guide to his own career. The profusion of animal figures can't help but lead one to the tale of Noah's Ark, even if they're not proceeding in twos. But of course the really striking image is Jackson's. There will be no more simple photographs of him on his album covers from *Dangerous* on; indexical, or "true", representations of him are gone, replaced by art that renders him increasingly removed from the human, increasingly mythological (he's a statue on the cover of *HIStory* and in part a digitally-created image on *Invincible*). Ryden makes him a cyborg (look at the image from a distance), with only his piercing, intense, seductive eyes—a look analogous to that surveilling moment in the "panther dance" when he gazes knowingly into the camera—and his jheri curl retained to let us know it's him. The center of his face, where his nose should be, is occupied by animals and golden cherubs, an effusive and beautiful rendering of the part of his body that was always under so much scrutiny. His gaping mouth, complete with fangs made out of statuary, reveals a factory, the tracks leading into and out of it, the tongue delivering up the factory's goods. As both Joe Vogel and Willa Stillwater note, the factory represents "inner workings," although each of them interprets these differently. My view is that the inner workings represent the private, linking the image to the tension between public and private found throughout the record; the metallic grey of the factory contrasts with the effusive color of the "exterior" and is meant to be viewed as cold, distant, and perhaps even threatening. As Stillwater notes, the album's title, DANGEROUS, is written directly over the image of the factory. This image vaguely alludes to Fritz Lang's film *Metropolis* and its horror of class struggle between wealthy industrialists and the (slave) labor on which their city is built. The cold, dark, grey, metallic, utilitarian image of the factory suggests the noisy, industrial sound of so much of the record, the disruption of the world, which sits at the center of the image, a disruption made by the oppressed or subjugated, including, of course, Jackson himself. It's unsurprising that the creation of this world would come through Jackson's throat—from the powerful instrument through which his ideas are made public.

I'm also reminded, while contemplating this painting, of Donna Haraway's influential "Cyborg Manifesto," because she talks about the transgression of boundaries between animal—or organism—and machine, between human and animal; even, invoking quantum physics, between the physical and non-physical as a reality of our contemporary existence, as much fact in our world (through advances in technology and medicine) as it might be science-fiction fantasy. But what's really important about her theory in this context is that in it the surrealists' vision has, at least in part, come true: these transgressions have done away with divisions between natural and artificial, mind and body, "self-developing and externally designed," as Haraway puts it. And, most importantly, she argues that the boundary transgressions bring us closer together, that they "signal disturbingly and pleasurably tight coupling" with others—all kinds of others.[6] In this sense, Ryden's painting beautifully captures the essence of what I would call Jackson's worldview, so much of which is about different kinds of kinship; I'd go so far as to call this a theology (it's no coincidence that a form—the Renaissance triptych—tied so closely to the sacred, is used to realize Ryden's surrealist vision). The over-arching thematic in Jackson's art and life is what has often been viewed as his "transgression" of normative boundaries—not only the most obvious of these—race and gender—but of generation, body morphology, divisions among species ("real" and fictional), artistic genres and technologies. Jackson moved so fluidly among performance traditions and subjectivities that he might productively be (re)thought through the lens of posthumanism in the sense that it calls into question liberal humanist ideas about the individual, unified, unchanging self, with the clear demarcation of boundaries between the human and non-human, between species and technologies. Cary Wolfe writes that we must acknowledge humans as "fundamentally prosthetic creature[s] that ha[ve] coevolved with various forms of technicity and materiality, forms that are radically 'not-human' and yet have nevertheless made the human what it is,"[7] and Jackson consistently and vividly called attention to, even celebrated this prosthetic idea of the human in specific ways. Through his plastic surgeries, shifting skin tones (lightening *and* darkening), gender/generation ambiguity (achieved partly through surgery, partly through fashion and make-up choices, partly through voice and gesture), through all of his fictional transformations—werewolf, zombie, panther, even a spaceship in *Moonwalker*—he held out his body not only as a work in progress, fully open to and trusting in limitless experimentation, but as part of a greater whole.

There's quite a long tradition of artists who have engaged in body modification as a way to test the limits of their flesh: among the most famous are Stelarc, whose projects have included *Ear on Arm*, an extra ear surgically-constructed on his forearm, an effort to "augment the body's forms and functions."[8] Or Orlan, a French artist, who in *The Reincarnation of Saint-Orlan*, used plastic surgery (nine times, to be exact, from 1990–5) to re-create her face in the image of famous paintings of women as idealized by male artists: it was intended as a feminist critique of art history, where women had long been "on the receiving end of the male gaze."[9] Perhaps Orlan's best known surgery involved having two little horns implanted on her forehead, just to mess with ideas of what constitutes a "normal" face. Jackson has been compared to Orlan before—mostly in an unfavorable way (her art is viewed as "political" and "self-conscious" whereas his is not). Jackson's body modifications are positively tame next to what these artists have done; they operate in the same and different realms simultaneously. Far from simply trying to look younger (or "white"), he set out to challenge ideas of gender, ethnicity and "normality" as these are written on the body, especially the face. But he did not do this in the unquestionably obvious ways that artists such as Orlan and Stelarc do. His manipulations were intended to be plausible, livable, to question boundaries of a more "everyday" kind, boundaries within which differently gendered and racialized people actually live. Unfortunately, he chose not to write manifestos about this, as Orlan has (her *Carnal Art Manifesto*[10]), or otherwise offer tremendously detailed explanations of what he was trying to do, as Stelarc has (visit his website). Commercial artists rarely talk about the intentions behind their work in the way that "experimental" or "avant-garde" artists do; and the commercialism tends to make us think that there is, in fact, little or no intention behind it. But in work as carefully crafted as Jackson's, including his body, this is just nonsense.

His queer ways of building kinship are extensions of the fluidity of his body. His family included animals, such as Bubbles the chimp, Muscles the snake and Louis the llama; I don't think it's accidental that Ryden placed so much emphasis on animals in his painting, including what is probably meant to be a representation of a crowned Bubbles at the very top and center, given how important they were to Jackson. One of the most significant images in the painting is the child—a black child—supported by Jackson's loving, but inanimate hand, even as he/she supports the animal skull. There is a lot of tenderness in those images, a lot of community among living and dead, animate and inanimate. His family also included Hollywood divas such as Elizabeth Taylor, as well as Frank Cascio's middle-class family from New Jersey. Cascio's father was manager of the Helmsley Palace in Manhattan; Jackson met and befriended him when he stayed at the hotel and essentially adopted the family as his own, regularly showing up and spending time at their home, vacuuming and making beds with his mother, according to Cascio's account, and hanging out with the kids.[11] His family also included children, of course, including but not limited to his own. His "entourage" at the 1984 Grammy Awards celebrated his ideas about non-normative kinship: Brooke Shields (beautiful white woman), child actor Emmanuel Lewis (black child), and Bubbles the chimp. I think were this to have taken place in the last few years, it would have been hailed as a serious challenge to dominant ideas of the "normal" nuclear family, which was much too small an idea of family for him. Much of this has been viewed as pathological and dangerous, especially by the media, because it was not a legible way of living, not legitimate, not "responsible;" kinship options outside of "normal" are, as philosopher Judith Butler writes "foreclosed as unthinkable … the terms of thinkability are enforced over the narrow debates about who and what will be included in the norm."[12] Jackson's vision of the body and kinship was actually forward looking, some might even say utopic. He modeled a way of being in the world that was predicated on the idea of what Haraway calls "affinity," not identity, on the creation of coalitions of the likeminded. I have a feeling that the various cherubs and skeletons in Ryden's painting fit effortlessly into Jackson's vision.

I say this because his boundary transgressions, especially in terms of kinship, map seamlessly onto his theology—no, not the Jehovah's Witness version his mother embraced. Around the time of *Bad*, Jackson befriended spiritual leader Deepak Chopra and the evidence of Chopra's influence starts to become especially prevalent with *Dangerous*. Chopra is often referred to as a "new age guru," but this reduces the complexity of his thought, which brings together a number of spiritual practices, including ancient Vedic texts, a spiritual tradition in which he was raised, with Western science (he's a medical doctor) and holistic medicine. Read Jackson's beautiful epigraph on the first page of the liner notes to *Dangerous*: dancing allows him to experience the sacred through merging with all creation, creation being the result of consciousness; creator and creation are one and the same. This echoes Chopra's fundamental spiritual message: "… the world is a seamless creation imbued with one intelligence, one creative design … . In the one reality, consciousness creates itself, which is the same as saying that God is inside his creation. There is no place outside creation for divinity to stand."[13] Chopra links this to quantum physics, which "reassembled time and space into a new geometry that has no beginning or end, no edges, no solidity … . The quantum field isn't separate from us—it is us. Where nature goes to create stars, galaxies, quarks and leptons, you and I go to create ourselves."[14] Everything, and everyone, therefore, is part of the whole and the divine, is inside, not outside this unity. Consciousness is creative, therefore we have the ability to influence it; our thoughts, as well as our actions, shape the world as well as the universe. Jackson had already explored these ideas before meeting Chopra, who has said that when he first visited Jackson's house, there were "little Krishna's all over."[15] In his work, these sentiments are expressed as far back as The Jacksons' "Can You Feel It," and also in "Another Part of Me" off the *Bad* album, both of which are certainly about unity and connection and exploding the myth of separation. But the public exploration of these ideas becomes central in the collection of poems and stories called *Dancing the Dream* that Jackson, with Chopra's help, published in 1992, and which is profoundly connected to *Dangerous*. The book begins with the words that grace the opening page of the liner notes to the album; the lyrics to "Heal the World" and "Will You Be There" are also reproduced. In page after page of this collection, Jackson turns to the themes of universal and timeless consciousness out of which we come and into which we return, the unity of this consciousness, the creative power of our thoughts; the ideas could come right out of one of Chopra's books—or those of fellow spiritual teachers such as Louise Hay, Eckhart Tolle, or *A Course in Miracles*. The poem "Heaven Is Here" offers one of the most fully worked out expressions of these ideas:[16]

> You and I were never separate
> It's just an illusion
> Wrought by the magical lens of
> Perception
>
> There is only one wholeness
> Only one Mind
> We are like ripples
> In the vast Ocean of Consciousness

But there are many other examples throughout *Dancing the Dream*: "Time, space, energy are just a notion, What we have conceptualized we have created." "Are you Listening: Immortality's my game, from Bliss I came, In Bliss I am sustained to Bliss I return … . This body of mine Is a flux of energy In the river of time, Eons pass, ages come and go, I appear and disappear." Jackson even links his artistic process to this idea: "People ask me how I make music. I tell them I just step into it. It's like stepping into a river and joining the flow."

The poems and reflections are accompanied by photographs, paintings, and drawings. The majority of the photos are of Jackson dancing. Of the 89 photographs in the book 36 come from the short film for "Black or White," including the cover photo. Most of these are stills taken from the "panther dance." This gives us some indication of how significant Jackson thought this piece was, and how, if it had to be excised from the film, he would make sure that parts of it lived on in this book. But it also, along with the myriad other photographs of him dancing, places that practice of his in the realm of the sacred, where, as he says, he becomes one with all creation.

*   *   *

Music is used in most cultures as a means through which to connect with the sacred, as a way to "heighten" the significance of words, to take them and our bodies out of the everyday, to re-fashion our sense of time and create community in a way that only music can do. There are so many different sacred music traditions; why draw on only one? Why not create crossover here, too? And in the process express, through musical sound, the theology of one consciousness?

The quartet of songs that follow "Black or White" trace a path of torturous personal struggle and quasi-redemption; for me, this "cluster" forms the heart and soul of the record. There is a profound turning inward. No more moralizing about the state of the world, no soul man machismo, no fraught utopias, no children—well, at least not until later. No noise, either. The first three songs display unmitigated and unhinged loneliness, despair, and longing, for which there appears to be little remedy. Like the "soul man" songs near the beginning of the album, most of these consciously undermine Jackson's brilliance for creating work that speaks multi-generationally, and so point, again, to this album as significantly different than previous offerings. This is where Jackson wrestles with adult demons, where he is betrayed, alone, and questions whether comfort and community are available to him at all. One of them on its own rips your heart out; but one was not enough. Jackson felt it necessary to pile on, to build the sense of despair over the course of three separate songs, each of which deploys a strikingly different musical language, some contemporary, some historical: what he seems to be saying is "I weep across religious affiliations and time." The fourth song, "Keep the Faith," attempts to lift us up from these depths, but although he tries hard to take us to church, I don't think the optimism is able to balance out the dread of what comes before it; not only that, but the song that follows, "Gone Too Soon," returns us to loss and despair. This song took on a particular meaning through the short film, which is dedicated to Ryan White, the teenage activist who contracted HIV/AIDS through blood trans-fusions he had to control his hemophilia; the fear and discrimination surrounding HIV/AIDS in the 1980s and early 1990s led to his expulsion from school for having the virus and media attention on White's case led to increased public awareness about its multiple causes. But on the album, there is no dedication of this song to White and so it's also possible to read it as a continuation of the general narrative of loss and loneliness that Jackson explores towards the end of the record.

"Who Is It" and "Give In To Me" are only about love of and betrayal by a woman on the surface; the lyrics are sufficiently vague to call the identity of Jackson's subject into question: "she" and "woman" can be viewed both as literal and metaphorical, about intimate relationships or relationships with the divine (I take my cue on this from Bono, who's often said that "she" in his lyrics refers to the Holy Spirit). I've wondered, for instance, if the "she" in "Who Is It," the "she" by whom the protagonist has been betrayed, is meant to signify the earthly church, by which promises were made and then broken. I've wondered if the burning desire felt in the chorus of "Give In To Me" is like that love the medieval mystics felt for Christ, described by them in erotic language (burning with desire was not an unusual metaphor) that tried to capture how powerfully they felt.

*　　*　　*

There was something about the sound of Gregorian Chant and pop culture in the early 1990s. The group Enigma released the album *MCMXC a.D.* in late 1990 and the single "Sadness, Part I," which incorporated the sacred chant, climbed to the top of the pop charts in over twenty countries. In the mid-1990s, a recording of Gregorian Chant made by the Monks of Santo Domingo de Silos in the 1970s was re-released and sold a phenomenal number of copies, mostly to yuppies who, as one newspaper cynically viewed it, used the music as "an antidote to stress."[17] Other recordings of chant-like music, such as *Vision: The Music of Hildegard of Bingen* (1994) combined sacred monophony with heavy beats, as Enigma had done a few years earlier, but released it under the name of the twelfth-century abbess and mystic herself.

Jackson frames and infuses "Who Is It" with chant, borrowing from the style, but not quoting directly. I don't know, of course, whether his allusion was conscious or not, but it's so close that it seems like it must have been. The opening angelic voices (one of those is, incredibly, his own) sing a simple phrase twice. This little phrase of music is modeled on the reciting tones of medieval chant, so-called because they were used to recite the Psalms, a form of prayer that lies at the heart of spiritual practice in the monastic tradition. There's also a nice allusion to the medieval in the "Who Is It" chant in that the harmony ends on the interval of the fourth—one of the most consonant intervals in the Middle Ages, but considered weird to more modern, Western ears. The "purity" of the voices (no vibrato, no distortion, straight and plain) and the enormous amount of reverb, which transports us to Notre Dame Cathedral or St. Mark's Basilica, also situate this music in the realm of the Christian sacred.

The groove of the song interrupts the chant/prayer: you think there might be another iteration of this beautiful melody, but instead you're jolted by a rhythmic language that comes from another world, but that retains traces of the chant motive: it may not be as noisy as earlier grooves on this record, but it's rhythmically sharp and dark, with the loud, driving bass very present on the first two beats of every bar—we're grounded by the bass in a way we weren't in earlier songs. Part of the struggle we hear in this song, musically, is that opening chant motive wanting to return against the forcefulness of the groove, and it tries in all kinds of guises: it returns on the third and fourth repetitions of the groove, before Jackson begins to sing, but it's been stripped of the nice little ornamental turn it had when we first heard it; it returns in this version during the choruses too. We hear it during the instrumental interlude, especially in the flute, where it's allowed to grow. And it appears in the cello, an instrument generally considered to have a mournful sound, at the end of the song. In fact that last time we hear the motive, on the cello, it reaches for the B♭, the lamenting sixth degree of the minor scale, before closing on the note below, not the tonic or home note of the scale, sounding unfinished. It seems pretty clear that the motive represents the sacred; the nature of this sacred—whether it's meant to comfort or terrorize—is unclear.

"Who Is It" is mesmerizing, not only because of the repetition of the motive throughout the piece, but also because of the chant-like qualities of other parts of the melody, especially that of the chorus with its stepwise motion and straight rhythm, and its incessant repetition in the last third of the song. There is also an epic and dark quality about the music: epic in the way the texture ebbs and flows through the different uses of the chant motive, constantly building to the high string orchestra sound. The straight, slow rhythm of the motive starts to sound eerily detached, somber but not able to match the emotional depths of Jackson's voice (particularly wounded here: one of the most touching moments comes when his otherwise exuberant "hee hee" is reduced to a pitiful sob; he could not have found a better means of conveying the profundity of his pain). That motive is meditative, but not particularly soothing. Too rigid, too structured, too inflexible, never able to recapture the simplicity and beauty of what we hear at the beginning. And at the end of the song the motive is abandoned, it just peters out, overtaken by Jackson's energetic beat boxing, which then also just fades out—not even a nice, long fade, but one that seems itself to be interrupted, cut off. All the striving for epic grandeur fizzles at the end of this song, it amounts to nothing.

*   *   *

Metal power ballads have been roundly criticized for their drippy sentimentality; largely responsible for bringing metal into the mainstream in the 1980s, such ballads were said by many to be "anthem[s] of commercial eagerness," and, perhaps worse in the minds of some misogynist fans and critics, that they were aimed at "Top 40 Housewives and their daughters,"[18] "watering down" the seriousness and power of the music. These ballads bring together elements thought to be incommensurable: the slow tempo, lyrical melodies, sense of intimacy, and expressive terrain that, as David Metzer puts it, "trades on love and loss"[19] found in traditional ballads—characteristics conventionally marked as more feminine, in musical terms—with the raw vocals, power chords and virtuosic guitar solos of rock and metal, which is often about machismo, power, sex, world-building, and control, not romanticism. The power ballad was there to celebrate romantic love: as revealed to a man by a woman (Foreigner's "I Want to Know What Love Is"), as a grounding effect of a woman on men who are "out in the world" (Guns N' Roses' "Sweet Child O Mine," Mötley Crüe's "Home Sweet Home"), as the acknowledgment that you (woman) were right and I (man) was wrong and I'm just so sorry now (Poison, "Every Rose Has Its Thorn," Whitesnake, "Is This Love"). Depending on how it's handled, the resulting intensity can either be unconvincingly saccharine or mind-blowingly effective, creating a kind of "energy into which listeners can disappear."[20]

Jackson harnesses the musical language and emotional intensity of the metal power ballad in "Give In To Me" to incredible effect, pushing emotional boundaries to their limits. But his aim is to mock the conventions of the genre, to, in his deep disillusionment, spit in the face of its treacly sentiments. The woman in his lyrics is brutal; she's not a source of comfort, doesn't represent "home," doesn't teach him the wonders of romantic love, doesn't tame his machismo or quench his desire. He's done nothing wrong, it seems, has nothing for which to repent (one of the things that women certainly responded to in other examples of this genre). There's heartache but no sentimentality. There's longing, but for sex, not romance. His grief and anger cause him to lash out—this is not supposed to happen in a power ballad.

The lyrics to this song have always seemed disjointed to me; it's worked better since I've given up trying to render them coherent. This is about feelings in turmoil; Jackson tries to capture that turmoil by expressing sorrow, hurt, defiance, anger, patience (never asking why) all at the same time. The feeling constantly shifts, as it does in tumultuous relationships. And there's a particular kind of disjuncture between the verses, where he appears to have mostly given up (especially clear in the defiant bridge, where he claims he won't any longer be around) and the chorus where he's demanding that his lover yield to his unrelenting desire. One of the most powerful things about the lyrics in the chorus is that every time we hear it some of the lines have shifted order, or a new line is introduced ("wrong" for a chorus), such an effective way to signal confusion, loss of control, being overcome, or overwrought: he can't keep things straight in his mind. The sound of his voice changes radically from verse to chorus: clean timbre, sliding up to notes to signal emotional excess, contrasted with loads of distortion and short, clipped phrases in the choruses.

One might think that such a song would continue to employ the device of musical groundlessness heard earlier on the album, but as with "Who Is It," that doesn't happen. Both verse and chorus use the same straightforward chord progression, the bass fully present and strong, the chords in root position. Coupled with the reverb-laden production that opens up musical space, especially the bottom end, this has the effect of drawing one into the pain: I feel those bass tones down in my soul. The progression does lend itself to ambiguity because it's easily possible to pivot from the dark minor mode to the sunny major mode—Patti Smith's "Because the Night" is a beautiful example of the way this can work to create contrast in mood—but Jackson doesn't allow for the play, doesn't open up that possibility, staying relentlessly in the minor mode.

As in so many of Jackson's songs, the chorus consumes the entire last half of the song, in this case drowning us—and the singer—in distortion, feedback, the majestic chords of the mellotron, and Slash's virtuosic and unbridled guitar solo. Slash was a brilliant choice for this song because his style of guitar playing favors emotional excess—that's a compliment—over clean, crisp technique. Yet this musical miasma somehow stays grounded and powerful because of the strong and conventional chord progression that undergirds both verse and chorus. Even when the progression stops, about a minute and fifteen seconds before the end of the song, it gives way to a grounding drone, on E, the tonic, doing away with the feeling of forward movement so that we can be fully present in the complexity and drama of the texture. The excesses of the song, and particularly the dramatic ending, are positively gothic.

As Joe Vogel notes, "Jackson had done rock before, but not like this."[21] There is none of the "theatricality," as Vogel calls it, of songs like "Beat It" or "Dirty Diana." What he wanted was the unrestrained emotional language, the grandeur, the epic quality of the metal ballad, not to celebrate love, but to lay bare the impossibility of the kind of love these ballads normally celebrate. Jackson has turned the dial just slightly from the chant-infused r&b world of "Who Is It" to the rock world of "Give In To Me," turned the musical language on its side a bit, given this theme another kick at the can, drilling down into the torrent of feelings, wringing out every last, exhausting drop of anguish, and finding that part of the depth of the betrayal is systemic/generic: even though he masters the genre, it's not for him. It leaves him hopelessly unfulfilled, with desire that burns, with no one to extinguish the flame, no matter how much he begs. White rock as religion, not an uncommon way of viewing it, isn't going lift him out of his despair, it's going to push him deeper into it (larger issues about race could certainly be read into this). Just like "Who Is It," "Give In To Me" fizzles out, the heavy groove reduced not, this time, to a single body beat boxing, but to a single line of guitar feedback, a sign of failure.

*   *   *

Jackson's quote from Beethoven's "Ode to Joy" at the beginning of "Will You Be There" may be "audacious" but it's not gratuitous.[22] The "Ode to Joy," which concludes the fourth movement of the Ninth Symphony, actually begins with text that the composer himself inserted before Schiller's poem: "Oh Friends, not these sounds. Let us instead strike up more pleasing and more joyful ones." It would have perhaps been too obvious for Jackson to quote these lines at the beginning of "Will You Be There," but his restless exploration of musical styles through which to express his soul-searching mirrors Beethoven's own in the finale of the Ninth. Beethoven revisits and then rejects musical ideas from previous movements of the symphony, and as is well known, this is the first symphony to employ voices, so Beethoven not only discards his own earlier ideas, but he rejects the conventional form of the genre in which he's composing, striking out on a new path, creating a new hybrid. Does this sound at all familiar?

Jackson *does* seem similarly to reject the musical genres, formal structures and spiritualities he's tried out so far on the album at this point, turning first to a high art tradition that lies miles outside the world of commercial pop music. The particular passage he's chosen from the "Ode to Joy" is perhaps the most deeply "religious" in a poem whose "religion" is usually celebrated for being of a secular kind, the "brotherhood of all mankind:"

> Do you bow down before him, you millions?
> Do you sense your Creator, World?
> Seek him above the starry firmament
> Above the stars he must dwell

Beethoven's music is reverential here, a huge contrast to what's come before and what comes directly afterwards: exuberance, break-neck tempos, crazy high soprano ranges belting out that well-known "Joy" theme with rhythmic certainty. This, in contrast, is a hymn, a pause for reflection; Beethoven directs the musicians to play it "with devoutness." What a striking choice for Jackson to make. The theology invoked here acknowledges a Creator, but not "God." It calls for the recognition of a higher power and for humility before it, but it's broadly enough construed that it could fit with Jackson's epigraph in the liner notes, with the sense of becoming one with the Creator and all creation. This is what Schiller calls for in his poem: "All men shall become brothers," and "Anyone who can call one soul his own on this earth [let him join our song of praise]." The poem has been called "a universal declaration of brotherhood," the final movement of the symphony "a quasi-religious yet non-denominational blessing on all 'good' and 'just' people and institutions."[23] This is all very close to the theology of "one consciousness" Jackson celebrates in *Dancing the Dream*, but of course Schiller's "Ode" also reflects Jackson's lifelong desire for peace and loving kindness in the world. To put this poem in its historical context, it was written at a time (the early nineteenth century) when, post-French Revolution, "terrified dynastic rulers strove to spruce up and enforce the concept of divine right." It was a moment characterized by "repression and ultraconservative nationalism."[24] Schiller's poem and Beethoven's setting of it spoke back to that repressiveness, to privilege by birth, to class separation, much in the way Jackson did throughout his life.

Yet the passage that Jackson quotes ends with uncertainty: the creator must dwell above the stars ... mustn't he? The music is questioning, too, ending on an unresolved chord that allows the question to hang in the air. In Beethoven's symphony, resolution comes in the following passage, but Jackson doesn't quote further; he just lets the question linger. "Will You Be There" is an exploration of this uncertainty, it's a direct plea to that creator who must surely be there, but might not be for him. The lovely choral passage that follows echoes the opening of "Who Is It," although a slightly different, if still archaic, musical language is invoked. It reminds me of Renaissance sacred polyphony, of one of Palestrina's masses, or Allegri's amazing "Miserere," with the soaring soprano line; the voices are reminiscent of the boys' choirs who sometimes sing this kind of music. Looks as though children start to return here as a sign of hope; after all, they appear in the short film for this song, actually singing (perhaps lip-synching) that opening angelic chorus.

At this reverential moment, Jackson turns away from the high art tradition to embrace the music of the black church, not in one song, but two, back to back. So much for the charges that he abandoned his black heritage. Here it becomes his salve, his home, his strength, his survival; it completes Beethoven, lest we think that Beethoven and the white high art tradition represent completion in and of themselves. He brings in the Andraé Crouch singers—the gospel choir, the whole community—to support him in both "Will You Be There" and "Keep the Faith." The choir doesn't offer a typical response to Jackson's call, but a series of imperatives, much like those in "Give In To Me." The community isn't just there to support, but to ask, with one voice, for healing, love, care, and blessing. In other words, it's not just Jackson who suffers, it's the community, and he's giving the community a voice.

Maybe questions aren't answered lyrically in "Will You Be There," but they are musically. The minor mode is left behind for a bright major key. Right from the entry of the piano there's a drone on the tonic that remains throughout much of the song, grounding us in the present moment. In fact, we never leave the tonic (home) in either the verses or the chorus (it gets embellished, but only during the bridge are there real structural chord changes). It's extraordinary to create a composition that more or less builds on a single chord. Jackson sings about an octave below his normal range for the first verse and a half (yes, he could sing down there), using a beautiful, warm, clear, open-throated timbre. He jumps up an octave to increase the intensity halfway through the second verse and this is where he stays for the rest of the song. The main device used to build the song is that modulation Jackson so loved. It's used no less than *three* times here, moving the piece from D major, to E, to F♯ and finally G♯ (A♭). That's a lot of rising up. And this is where the song ends—we don't come back to the beginning, we've landed, fully, in this new key, this new territory. Risen up to it. The opening "angelic" chorus that I thought sounded like Renaissance polyphony is also recapped near the end of the song, after the exuberant chorus stops singing words and we have an instrumental interlude with the chorus humming: that "Renaissance" choral opening has now been fully embraced by the language of gospel, has reconfigured and grounded that somewhat distant, reverb-drenched sound associated with another Christian tradition. Jackson has not yet found comfort, however; in fact, he's reduced to speaking, something we rarely hear him do. This prayer—I think we can call it that—reaches into the dark corners of being human. I think Jackson's acknowledgment of the "violence(s)" we commit is particularly noteworthy and an unusual but perspicuous inclusion in a pop song that elevates the other emotions and states he describes out of banal sentimentality.

*   *   *

I've wanted to dig into the music of these three songs because Jackson has, with such a deft hand, made his spiritual journey here in large part through invoking so many musical languages. His musical journey is a metaphor for spiritual seeking. I've barely touched on the short films, one made for each of these songs. I have to say that in my humble opinion, these films don't do the music justice. It makes complete sense that for "Give In To Me" he would have set the video at a concert, since this is the most authentic choice for rock and metal videos, where a demonstration of the musicians' skills in live performance is of paramount importance. This also gave him the opportunity to feature Slash in the video, which, given that Guns N' Roses were, if not quite at their peak, then still pretty significantly at the height of their popularity, lent Jackson considerable credibility with an audience that otherwise probably didn't listen to his music. But the parallel narrative of conventional couples' turmoil seems too simplistic for a Jackson film and dilutes the power both of the lyric and the music. And while Jackson is portrayed as lonely in the short film for "Who Is It," revisiting the *femme fatale* theme seems to trivialize the depth of despair Jackson explores in the song. It's entirely possible that what I'm truly missing is Jackson's dancing body, which is why the short film for "Will You Be There" is, I think, the most successful of the three. The beautiful and sensuous choreography, complete with the acting out of a story—really about the sharing and reclamation of the globe (a return of that important symbol) and what looks like a sacred book. Africa makes another appearance in this film in the costumes of the dancers—Jackson seems to have been determined to give the continent presence throughout these years.

It's an otherwise haphazard film, cutting from the 1991 MTV Video Awards performance of the song to concert footage, footage of fans and Jackson among his fans. Other than the dancing, I've always been struck by the presence of the car in the segments of the film that are taken from the MTV performance. That car is there because the song performed just prior to "Will You Be There" was "Black or White." Despite the controversy over the "panther dance" that had ensued with the premiere of the short film only two weeks earlier, Jackson performed it on the awards show, complete with the car, which he dances on top of, although he doesn't perform the whole "panther dance." I think that would have been too simple a dare for Jackson. Instead, he turns this performance of the song into an all-out metal fest and once again manipulates musical genre to make a point. Slash performs with him and *he's* left to kick the offending trash can off the stage and to drive his guitar into the car at the end of the performance. Maybe Jackson was making the point that in rock 'n' roll gratuitous violence (which is what this amounts to here, as opposed to the short film for "Black or White") is perfectly acceptable, even cheered on; why can Slash get away with it when he couldn't? Why is rock 'n' roll rebellion of a general sort cool, but rebellion against racism taboo? The rap section of the song is completely excised in order to make lots of space for Slash's virtuosic exhibition, but what does this do to the beautiful symmetry of the song, and the bringing together of disparate musical genres to make a point about racial harmony? Gone. Perhaps the most extraordinary moment, though, occurs after this extravagant display is over. Jackson begins "Will You Be There" leaning up against the car. As if to reclaim the subversive culture of graffiti art from its questionable appropriation in the edited version of "Black or White"—the hideous racial slurs—Jackson leans up against a car that is entirely covered in graffiti. The camera circles over the top of the car to reveal a single slogan written on the hood: "women's rights now."

*   *   *

Jackson "wrestl[ed] with religiously informed, morally shaped, and culturally conditioned themes" throughout his work, wrote Michael Eric Dyson in 1993; these themes form what Dyson called Jackson's "own vision of African-American spirituality."[25] This group of songs on *Dangerous* offers one of the most sustained and capacious expressions of Jackson's spiritual struggles, his wrestling with religion, the soul, betrayal, and redemption; serious, adult stuff. What Jackson does so remarkably well—here, yes, but everywhere in his performances—is offer us catharsis, which Dyson argues is part of the spiritual significance of his performances and which "creates space for cultural resistance and religious agency."[26] Jackson knew how powerful this kind of cathartic performance could be, saying in 2007 that this was precisely what was so compelling to him about James Brown: "He would give a performance that would just exhaust you, just wear you out emotionally. His whole physical presence, the fire coming out of his pores, would be phenomenal. You'd feel every bead of sweat on his face, and you'd know what he was going through."[27] That's what Jackson aspired to give his audience—he became a conduit for release of all kinds, release that can be thought of in spiritual terms. Interestingly, part of what Jackson achieves in this group of songs—also expressed in Ryden's cover art—is to bring high and low art traditions together, giving us yet another example of his desire for crossover, this one not about commercial viability, but social unity.

Coda

Dangerous

In some ways, "Gone Too Soon" seems to wrap up the main narrative of this record. It just feels like a conclusion to all the soul searching that's preceded it, a beautiful but pained letting go, a surrender. Maybe it strikes me this way because Jackson paints with the same open, emotional palette that he's used throughout much of the album: he's vulnerable, exposed; his pristine tenor—harkening back to a track like "She's Out of My Life"—far forward in the mix. Once again, this song is so stylistically different and the sound of Jackson's voice so removed from anything else on the album that one marvels at the possibility of its appearance. Although it would have been a real downer, the album could have ended here.

But of course it doesn't. Jackson decides to take us back to the beginning, to come full circle, ending stylistically where he began, returning not only to noise and a hard-hitting, industrial Teddy Riley groove, but back to his breath, the first sound he makes on this record. What an ingenious way to connect the dots. Those sharp expulsions of breath we hear at the beginning of "Jam" not only return in "Dangerous," but become something of a sonic principle, linking and developing the embodied intensity of one song to another, seventy-odd minutes down the road. About three and a half minutes into "Dangerous" there's an eight-bar break that features Jackson's hard exhalations, brilliantly placed on beats one and three—the "strong" beats of the bar, not the backbeat. They hit those beats hard and dead in the center. They're solid, stable, deliberately placed, just as they were in "Jam." This is one of the most intense moments I've ever encountered on a record: those breaths just keep coming, on and on, an encapsulation of Jackson's incredible intensity as a performer, of his body *as* rhythm, groove. His breath, this time even sharper and pitched lower, grunts and growls throughout the long outro to the song, and the record. It comes from and exposes his embodied depths, the "inner workings." Breath is intimate. Breath, the thing we live by and through, frames this record; breath that is forced, sharp, labored, heavy, hungry.

It's not as though "Dangerous" lifts us out of the pain of "Gone Too Soon" in the way that "Keep the Faith" attempted to after the trio of soul-searching songs that preceded it. It's more of a left turn than that, at once removed from and picking up on narrative threads. It functions as a coda to the record, moving Jackson away from the emotional openness, the "realness" that he has offered throughout, back into his world of stylized theatricality and the utilitarian genre of dance music. But it also returns us to the central theme of noise as disruption, which was left behind with "Black or White."

I'm reminded of *Sgt. Pepper's* again. On that record, the title (and opening) song is reprised; it's transformed from a big orchestral piece to a stripped down, faster, straight-ahead rock 'n' roll number. Musical symmetry dictates that it should be the last song on the record—you recap, you end—but instead, it's followed by "A Day in the Life," a song that, as Tim Riley put it, thrusts the listener out of the fantasy world produced over the course of the record back into "the parallel universe of everyday life … redefining everything that came before."[1] I think it works in a more complex way on *Dangerous*: lyrically and emotionally, the last track is a retreat from reality, from real-world problems, into theatricality, to the presentation of stylized, more two-dimensional characters, a tough-guy barrier that safely distances Jackson from the world of hurt he has explored throughout the record. But musically, the reappearance of noise and a heavy industrial groove signals a return to the fight, to disruption, to agitation of the status quo; his breath is part of the noise—growling, grunting, sharp exhalations of breath. Who needs words to convey the idea that you're out to create trouble?

But lyrically, this track also complicates the idea that *he* is dangerous, because wouldn't you know, just when we're sure that the record's title was meant to refer to Jackson, it turns out that this adjective describes a woman, one of Jackson's *femmes fatales*; he uses this neat double entendre trick on *Invincible* too—it's not him, or at least not only him, who's invincible, but his lover. It's in part these *femme fatale* songs, which include "Billie Jean," "Dirty Diana" and the *really* dangerous and violent "Susie" in "Blood on the Dance Floor," that have made critics conclude that he feared women and viewed them as a threat, even though there are plenty of other kinds of love songs in his recorded output, including earlier offerings on *Dangerous*. Nevertheless, he did like to return to this theme. What did he find so compelling about it? And why are these among the songs I love most in his repertory? This does nothing whatsoever for my feminist credentials.

Jackson's *femmes fatales* are mostly situated within a cinematic musical narrative, and it's clear that his interest in this character came out of his love of classic Hollywood movies. In fact, some of the lyrics to the verses in "Dangerous" are lifted directly out of "The Girl Hunt Ballet" in Fred Astaire's movie *The Bandwagon*.[2] (The lines in the film are: "She came at me in sections, more curves than a scenic railway. She was bad, she was dangerous. I wouldn't trust her any farther than I could throw her.") Surely Jackson's reference to this narrative in "Dangerous" is what led him to speak the words of the verses in his low (yes, low), seductive voice, mimicking Astaire's tough-guy detective character in *Bandwagon*. Astaire doesn't sound nearly as sexy as Jackson. Astaire's going to stay the tough, detached, stock character detective guy, hear? Jackson is lost in the seduction and weirdly, perhaps, he doesn't sound so much tough guy as seducer himself. In fact come to think of it, *he* sounds like the *femme fatale*, despite what he's saying. Nothing was ever very simple with him.

Jackson's *femmes fatales* songs all have different narratives and are worthy of a good and thorough study, which is more than I can do here. There's a long tradition in literature, cinema, opera and popular music (heavy metal of the 1980s in particular) of these characters—most of them created by dudes who viewed women as a serious threat—who use their potent sexual allure to rope "hapless" men into various situations that compromise their power. The women in these stories have often needed to be killed in order to eradicate their threat. It's a problematic and often misogynistic construction, and we can't exempt Jackson from taking it up in some disturbing ways. In my (perhaps feeble) defense, it's the wicked grooves, his voice and his seductive confidence that bring me back to these songs, not the lyrics which, as is the often the case in popular music, one can take or leave. But also, Jackson's *femmes fatales* don't end up victims; they get away with their seductions. They're pretty powerful women: tough girls. And in "Blood on the Dance Floor," there's a moral to the story: it's one-night stands, sex without romance or love that gets the protagonist of the story—and over-heated men who can't control themselves in general—into trouble, although it's still unclear why this morality tale needs to be told on the back of a woman drawn as vicious and violent.

"Dangerous" is one of Jackson's most ambiguous *femme fatale* songs. One of the most interesting lines of the lyric is this: "her inner spirit was as sharp as a two-edged sword, but I loved it 'cause it's dangerous." So on the one hand, we get the typical *femme fatale* narrative about a man feeling afraid, trapped, and manipulated by a powerfully seductive woman, but on the other, he admits to loving it *because* it's dangerous. This is quite a revealing idea and, although I'm wary of mapping everything in Jackson's art onto his biography, it fits, doesn't it? He did like dangerous things, did like pushing all kinds of limits and boundaries. The sentiment is taken up in a stunning live performance of the song at the 1995 MTV Music Video Awards, where after a medley of some of his greatest hits, he says to the audience: "Listen, some of us like to play it safe and take each day as it comes; some of us like to take that crazy walk on the wild side. So for those of us who like living dangerously, this one's for you." The performance is one of Jackson's most complex choreographed group dances, even outdoing "Smooth Criminal," a small portion of which is incorporated, connecting the two songs through the "gangster" narrative, a narrative that Jackson also returned to throughout his career and one that complicates his soft spokenness off stage in the same way that his soul man machismo did; he's a pretty cool and seductive crook. And certainly part of his project must have been to demonstrate that a black man could inhabit that kind of powerful character as convincingly as white men had (even as he had appropriated the white thriller genre earlier in his career); we now celebrate the fact that black actors take on lead roles in action films, don't we, even though some of the narratives in those films are excessively violent or misogynistic?

In the MTV performance, Jackson speaks the opening lyric with little musical accompaniment; the groove kicks in and he begins to dance after the line "divinity in motion." This now refers to him, since what follows is exactly that. Not only is he a dangerous character—assuming the gangster stance and all—but his virtuosity as a dancer renders him super human, simultaneously all control, precision, sensuousness, and seduction. At one point the music stops and in a small, taunting, gender-ambiguous voice he says to his audience "You know you want me." It's unclear whether this voice is even his, since he's lip-synching. Who wants whom? Who's talking, who's desiring?

*   *   *

Alan Light's description of Jackson at his best—"sexually charged, tense, coiled"—holds from beginning to end of this album, with the closing track among the finest examples of this. After coming through the record we could add that he was at his best when he was politically engaged and questioning, spiritually hungry, interested in social justice. He did this on *Dangerous* by digging deeper than he had before into the musical well—and that's saying something—not only drawing on and mastering more available musical styles than seems humanly possible just because as a virtuosic musician he could, but because this became part of a politics.

Dangerous is a monumental album. It's Jackson as a fully mature artist, no longer content with astronomical commercial success, ready to launch himself into the minefields of contemporary politics and subjectivities. Armond White's comment about Jackson's career as a whole is particularly apt for *Dangerous* and the work that came after it: "MJ's importance wasn't showbiz as usual, it moved through the ongoing issues of race, class, sex, law, spirituality and aesthetics … . As time has shown, *Thriller* wasn't the culmination of Jackson's career [which is what] his disengaged eulogizers now claim … . Perhaps

Jackson's movements came too fast for the cultural gatekeepers."[3]

Or perhaps they just couldn't see the significance of his later artistic movements, paralyzed by Wittgenstein's "mental picture" that "held them captive," by the relentless media fabrications and bullying that simply drowned out his mature work. Or, most probably, the new politically conscious art that he was creating and the increasingly gender- and racially-ambiguous, sexy, grown-up image he presented to the world was too threatening to tolerate. It seems to have taken his death to begin, slowly, to remove the veil, to silence—or at least curtail—the tabloid noise, and take another listen.

Notes

Introduction

1   Ludwig Wittgenstein, *Philosophical Investigations*, G. E. M. Anscombe (trans.) (Oxford: Blackwell, 1958), §115.

2   Alan Light, Michael Jackson: *Dangerous*, *Rolling Stone*, January 1, 1992. http://www.rollingstone.com/music/albumreviews/dangerous-19920101

3   Jon Dolan, "King of Pain," *Rolling Stone Special Commemorative Issue: Michael Jackson*, 2009, 68.

4   Joseph Vogel, "Dangerous, Nevermind, and the Reinvention of Pop," *Featuring Michael Jackson: Collected Writings on the King of Pop* (New York: Baldwin Books, 2012), 30–1.

5   Nelson George, *Thriller: The Musical Life of Michael Jackson* (Cambridge, MA: Da Capo Press, 2010), 196–7.

6   Vogel, "Dangerous," 35.

7   Armond White, *Keep Moving: The Michael Jackson Chronicles* (New York: Resistance Works, 2009), 68.

8   Joseph Vogel, *Man in the Music: The Creative Life and Work of Michael Jackson* (New York: Sterling), 20–1.

9   Bill Wyman, "The Pale King: Michael Jackson's Ambiguous Legacy," *The New Yorker*, December 24, 2012. http://www.newyorker.com/arts/critics/books/2012/12/24/121224crbo_books_wyman

10 George, *Thriller*, 85.

11 Dave Marsh, *Trapped: Michael Jackson and The Crossover Dream* (New York: Bantam, 1985). Final chapter reprinted here: http://www.counterpunch.org/2009/08/28/trapped-again/

12 Cornel West, "Black Postmodernist Practices: Interview with Anders Stephanson," *The Cornell West Reader* (New York: Civitas Books), 288.

13 http://video.pbs.org/video/1169160819/

14 Booth Moore, "'Herb Ritts L.A. Style' at Getty with Fashion, Celeb Photographs," *Los Angeles Times*, April 4, 2012. http://latimesblogs.latimes.com/alltherage/2012/04/herb-ritts-la-style-opens-at-the-getty-with-fashion-celebrity-photographs-1.html

15 Ben Beaumont-Thomas, "*Dangerous* was Michael Jackson's True Career High," *The Guardian Music Blog*, Monday, July 6, 2009. http://www.guardian.co.uk/music/musicblog/2009/jul/06/michael-jackson-dangerous

16 Light, *Michael Jackson*.

17 Michael Awkward, "A Slave to the Rhythm: Essential(ist) Transmutations; or The Curious Case of Michael Jackson," *Negotiating Difference: Race, Gender and the Politics of Positionality* (Chicago: University of Chicago Press, 1995), 191.

Noise

1   Jacques Attali, *Noise: The Political Economy of Music* (Minneapolis: University of Minnesota Press, 1985), 1.

2   Elizabeth Chin, "Michael Jackson's Panther Dance: Double Consciousness and the Uncanny Business of Performing While Black," *Journal of Popular Music Studies* 23/1 (2011): 70.

3   Dick Hebdige, *Subculture: The Meaning of Style* (London: Routledge, 1979).

4   Luigi Russolo, *The Art of Noises: Futurist Manifesto 1913*, Robert Filliou (trans.) (New York: Something Else Press, 1967).

5   Robert Walser, "Rhythm, Rhyme and Rhetoric in Public Enemy," *Ethnomusicology* 39/2 (1995): 197.

6   Tricia Rose, *Black Noise: Rap Music and Black Culture in Contemporary America* (Middletown, CT: Wesleyan University Press, 1994), 62.

7   Ibid.

8   Walser, "Rhythm," 197.

9   Jackson's long-time recording engineer, Bruce Swedien, commented that "Michael... loves to experiment with sound … ." Swedien, *In the Studio With Michael Jackson* (Milwaukee: Hal Leonard Books, 2009), 19.

10 Bill Wyman, "The Pale King: Michael Jackson's Ambiguous Legacy," *The New Yorker*, December 24, 2012.

11 Willa Stillwater, "Jam Revisited," *M Poetica: Michael Jackson's Art of Connection and Defiance* (Kindle Editions, 2011).

12 Nelson George, *Post Soul Nation* (New York: Penguin, 2004), 68.

13 David Harvey, *A Brief History of Neoliberalism* (Oxford: Oxford University Press, 2005), 3.

14 David Brackett, "Black or White: Michael Jackson and the Idea of Crossover," *Popular Music and Society* 35/2 (2012): 178.

15 Thanks to Timmy Mo for these thoughts about "Man in the Mirror."

16 Lawrence Kramer, *Classical Music and Postmodern Knowledge* (Berkeley: University of California Press, 1995), 9.

17 Frederic Jameson, *Postmodernism, or the Cultural Logic of Late Capitalism* (New York: Verso, 1991), 9.

18 M. G. Durham and Douglas Kellner, *Media and Cultural Studies Keyworks* (Malden: MA: Blackwell, 2001), 514.

19 Ibid.

20 Cornel West, "Black Culture and Postmodernism," *A Postmodern Reader*, Joseph Natoli and Linda Hutcheson (eds) (Albany: The State University of New York, 1993), 393.

21 bell hooks, "Postmodern Blackness," *A Postmodern Reader*, 510–18.

22 Michele Wallace, "Michael Jackson, Black Modernisms and the 'Ecstasy of Communication,'" *Invisibility Blues: From Pop to Theory* (New York: Verso, 1990), 78–9.

23 hooks, "Postmodern Blackness," 514–15.

24 bell hooks, *Yearning: Race, Gender and Cultural Politics* (New York: South End Press, 1990), 4.

25 Willa Stillwater also discusses the politics of "jamming" in the short film for "Jam" in her book *M Poetica*.

26 Armond White, *Keep Moving: The Michael Jackson Chronicles* (New York: Resistance Works, 2009), 42.

27 George made this comment in Spike Lee's documentary film *Bad 25* (Forty Acres and a Mule Productions, 2012).

Desire

1 http://www.youtube.com/watch?v=hiKbz6RCPfw

2 For a montage, go here: http://www.youtube.com/watch?v=Th1hBKI5DDQ

3 Reported in Examiner.com http://www.examiner.com/article/madonna-talks-michael-jackson-rolling-stone-i-was-madly-love-with-him-totally-smitten

4 Julie-Ann Scott, "Cultural Anxiety Surrounding a Plastic Prodigy: A Performance Analysis of Michael Jackson as an Embodiment of Post-Identity Politics," *Michael Jackson: Grasping the Spectacle*, Christopher R. Smit (ed.) (London: Ashgate, 2012), 173.

5 Jay Cocks, quoted in Dave Marsh, *Trapped: Michael Jackson and The Crossover Dream* (New York: Bantam, 1985), 110.

6 Ibid.

7 Mark Fisher (ed.), *The Resistible Demise of Michael Jackson* (Winchester: O Books, 2009), 14.

8 Margo Jefferson, *On Michael Jackson* (New York: Vintage, 2006), 97.

9 Reid Kane, "The King of Pop's Two Bodies," in Mark Fisher (ed.), *The Resistible Demise of Michael Jackson*, 234.

10 Randall Sullivan, *Untouchable: The Strange Life and Tragic Death of Michael Jackson* (New York: Grove Press, 2012).

11 As Willa Stillwater noted to me in a conversation, terms like "man-child" and "man boy" also have racial overtones, much like calling a black man "boy" in order to demean and render him powerless.

12 http://www.robertchristgau.com/get_album.php?id =2375

13 Jon Pareles, "Michael Jackson in the Electronic Wilderness," *The New York Times*, November 24, 1991. http://www.nytimes.com/1991/11/24/arts/recordings-view-michael-jackson-in-the-electronic-wilderness. html

14 Joseph Vogel, "I Ain't Scared of No Sheets," *A History That Doesn't Go Away: Race, Masculinity and Representation in the American Imaginary* (Doctoral Dissertation, University of Rochester, 2014).

15 Mark Anthony Neal, *Looking for Leroy: Illegible Black Masculinities* (New York: New York University Press, 2013), 143.

16 See Neal's comments here: http://www.youtube. com/watch?v=WLGnyva6_4s

17 http://www.youtube.com/watch?v=gVps8jOl91Q

18 Thanks to Amy Verhaeghe for her comments on Campbell and race in the short film. The idea of Jackson as racially other to Campbell in this film is Willa Stillwater's http://dancingwiththeelephant.

wordpress.com/2012/08/08/summer-rewind-series-week-7-in-the-closet/

19 Herb Ritts interview on Entertainment Tonight, 1992: http://michaelerz.tumblr.com/post/25782064765/in-the-closet-some-insights-from-co-star-naomi

20 Stacey Appel, *Michael Jackson Style* (London: Omnibus, 2012), 130.

21 Mark Anthony Neal, *Songs in the Keys of Black Life: A Rhythm and Blues Nation* (New York: Routledge, 2003), 44.

22 Harriet Manning also makes this argument, through an analysis of "Scream" in which Jackson's voice is compared to his sister's. Harriet Manning, *Michael Jackson and the Blackface Mask* (London: Ashgate, 2013), 157.

23 Jacqueline Warwick, "You Can't Win, Child, but You Can't Get Out of the Game: Michael Jackson's Transition from Child Star to Superstar," *Popular Music and Society* 35/2 (May 2012): 255.

24 Willa Stillwater, *M Poetica: Michael Jackson's Art of Connection and Defiance* (Kindle Edition, 2011), and "Monsters, Witches and Michael Jackson's Ghosts" (unpublished article).

25 Meredith Jones, "Makeover Artists: Orlan and Michael Jackson," *Skintight: An Anatomy of Cosmetic Surgery* (New York: Bloomsbury Academic, 2008), 164.

26 Michael Bush, *The King of Style: Dressing Michael Jackson* (New York: Insight Editions, 2012), 136.

27 Jefferson, *On Michael*, 102.

28 Vogel, "Sheets."

29 Thanks to Justin Raymond for these thoughts.

30 David Brown, "Michael Jackson's Black or White Blues," *Entertainment Weekly*, November 29, 1991. http://www.ew.com/ew/article/0,,20396305_316363,00.html

31 Thanks to the students in my MJ seminar for helping me work through these ideas. Manning makes a case for thinking about Jackson through the lens of transvestism, not in terms of cross-dressing, but more subtly, through behavior, facial appearance, etc. See Manning, Chapter 7.

32 Judith Peraino, *Listening to the Sirens: Musical Technologies of Queer Identity from Homer to Hedwig* (Berkeley: University of California Press, 2005), 227–8.

33 George makes this point in Spike Lee's film *Bad 25*.

34 John Singleton, "Like My Big Brother," *Michael Jackson Opus* (Guernsey: Kraken Sports and Media, 2009), 200.

35 Michael Bush, *The King of Style*: *Dressing Michael Jackson* (San Raphael, CA: Insight Editions, 2012), 146.

36 *An Introduction to the History and Culture of Pharaonic Egypt*. http://www.reshafim.org.il/ad/egypt/index.html

37 Thanks to Stan Hawkins for his helpful suggestions in this analysis.

38 Henry Louis Gates, *The Signifying Monkey: A Theory of African-American Literary Criticism* (New York: Oxford University Press, 1989), 6.

39 Gates, *Signifying Monkey*, 29.

40 Gates, *Signifying Monkey*, 6.

41 Gates, *Signifying Monkey*, 29.

42 Quoted in Gates, *Signifying Monkey*, 29.

43 Gates, *Signifying Monkey*, 29.
44 "Two Spirited People of the First Nations." Rainbow Resource Centre, Manitoba. www.rainbowresource centre.org
45 "Karen Faye, Dennis Thompkins, Michael Bush on ABC 20/20," June 25, 2010 http://www.youtube.com/watch?v=-OfT8uNHmuI
46 Stan Hawkins, *The British Pop Music Dandy* (London: Ashgate, 2009), 21.
47 Stan Hawkins and Sarah Niblock, *Prince: The Making of a Pop Music Phenomenon* (London: Ashgate, 2011), 47.
48 Wallace, quoted in Vogel, "Sheets."
49 Monica L. Miller, *Slaves to Fashion: Black Dandyism and the Styling of Black Diasporic Identity* (Durham, NC: Duke University Press, 2009), 87.
50 Miller, *Slaves to Fashion*, 82.
51 Miller, *Slaves to Fashion*, 84.
52 Miller, *Slaves to Fashion*, 85.
53 Bush, *The King of Style*, 63.
54 Bush, *The King of Style*, 8.
55 Bush, *The King of Style*, 63.
56 Bush, *The King of Style*, 40.
57 Miller, *Slaves to Fashion*, 93.
58 Quoted in Appel, *Style*, 130.

Utopia

1 Michael Jackson, *Moonwalk* (New York: Harmony Books, 1988), 282.
2 José Muñoz, *Cruising Utopia: The Then and There of Queer Futurity* (New York: New York University Press, 2009), 10.

3   Richard Dyer, "Entertainment and Utopia," *Only Entertainment*, Richard Dyer (ed.) (London: Routledge, 1992), 20.

4   Ibid.

5   Dyer, "Entertainment and Utopia," 26.

6   Michael Bush, *The King of Style: Dressing Michael Jackson* (New York: Insight Editions, 2012), 162.

7   The entire short text can be found here: http://www.cbsnews.com/8301-504803_162-57585206-10391709/mjs-manifesto-penned-in-1979/

8   Muñoz, *Cruising*, 11.

9   Jill Dolan, *Utopia In Performance: Finding Hope at the Theater* (Ann Arbor: University of Michigan Press, 2005), 5–6.

10   Quoted in Muñoz, *Cruising*, 5.

11   Steven Shaviro, "Pop Utopia: The Promise and Disappointment of Michael Jackson," *The Resistible Demise of Michael Jackson*, Mark Fisher (ed.) (Washington: O Books, 2009), 56.

12   "Online Audio Chat, October 26, 2001," moderated by Anthony DeCurtis (transcript). http://www.allmichaeljackson.com/interviews/onlineaudiochat.html

13   Vogel mentions this, *Man in The Music, The Creative Life and Work of Michael Jackson* (New York: Sterling, 2011), 157.

14   Joseph Vogel, "I Ain't Scared of No Sheets," *A History That Doesn't Go Away: Race, Masculinity and Representation in the American Imaginary* (Doctoral Dissertation, University of Rochester, 2014).

15   Tavia Nyong'o, "Have You Seen His Childhood?," *Journal of Popular Music Studies* 23/1 (2011): 41.

16 Armond White, *Keep Moving: The Michael Jackson Chronicles* (New York: Resistance Works, 2009), 22.

17 For more on the idea of childhood, hope and futurity see Peter Kraft, "Young People, Hope and Childhood Hope," *Space and Culture* 11/2 (May 2008): 81–92.

18 Michael Jackson, "Wise Little Girl," *Dancing the Dream: Poems and Reflections* (New York: Doubleday, 1992), 99.

19 Judith Halberstam, *In a Queer Time and Place: Transgender Bodies, Subcultural Lives* (New York: New York University Press, 2005), 4–5.

20 Susan McClary, *Conventional Wisdom: The Content of Musical Form* (Berkeley: University of California Press, 2001), 5–6.

21 See Gates, *The Signifying Monkey: A Theory of African-American Literary Criticism* (New York: Oxford University Press, 1989). Joe Vogel also connects "Black or White" to the practice of signifying in "I Ain't Scared of No Sheets."

22 David Bracket, "Black or White: Michael Jackson and the Idea of Crossover," *Popular Music and Society* 35/2 (2012): 173–4.

23 Lisha McDuff, "I'd Rather Hear Both Sides of the Tale," *Dancing with the Elephant* Blog https://dancing-withtheelephant.wordpress.com/2012/04/25/id-rather-hear-both-sides-of-the-tale/

24 See my article "Michael Jackson's Queer Musical Belongings," *Popular Music and Society* 35/2 (2012): 281–300.

25 See Vogel, *Man in the Music*, 159.

26 Vogel, "Sheets."

27 Ibid.

28 Willa Stillwater, "You're Just Another Part of Me: Smooth Criminal," *M Poetica: Michael Jackson's Art of Connection and Defiance* (Kindle Edition, 2011).

29 Vogel, "Sheets."

30 Eric Lott, "The Aesthetic Ante: Pleasure, Pop Culture and The Middle Passage," *Callaloo* 17/2 (1994): 553.

31 Thanks to Lisha McDuff for complicating the reading of this scene.

32 Vogel, "Sheets."

33 Elizabeth Chin, "Michael Jackson's Panther Dance: Double Consciousness and the Uncanny Business of Performing While Black," *Journal of Popular Music Studies* 23/1 (2011): 60.

34 Chin, "Panther Dance," 61.

35 White, "Keep Moving," 26.

36 Lisha McDuff, *I'd Rather Hear Both Sides of the Tale: Adorno's Two Spheres and Michael Jackson's "Black or White."* (M.A. thesis, University of Liverpool, 2013).

37 Michel Foucault, *Discipline and Punish: The Birth of the Prison* (New York: Random House, 1975).

38 I am indebted to Willa Stillwater for pointing me in the direction of "Limehouse Blues" and its connection to "Black or White." For more on this connection, see http://dancingwiththeelephant.wordpress.com/2013/11/07/fred-astaire-and-the-real-limehouse-blues/

39 Chin, "Panther Dance," 72.

Soul

1 Joseph Vogel, *Man in the Music: The Creative Life and Work of Michael Jackson* (New York: Sterling, 2011), 145.

2   Vogel, *Man in the Music*, 146.
3   Louise Tyathcott, *Surrealism and the Exotic* (New York: Routledge, 2003), 1.
4   Quoted in Tyathcott, 2.
5   Many thanks to Lisha McDuff for suggesting this reading.
6   Donna Haraway, "A Manifesto for Cyborgs: Science, Technology and Socialist Feminism in the 1980s," *Feminism/Postmodernism*, Linda J. Nicholson (ed.) (London: Routledge, 1990), 193–4.
7   Cary Wolfe, *What is Posthumanism?* (Minneapolis: University of Minnesota Press, 2009), xxv.
8   http://stelarc.org/?catID=20229
9   Stuart Jefferies, "Orlan's Art of Sex and Surgery," *The Guardian*, July 1, 2009. http://www.theguardian.com/artanddesign/2009/jul/01/orlan-performance-artist-carnal-art
10   http://orlan.eu/adriensina/manifeste/carnal.html
11   Frank Cascio, *My Friend Michael* (New York: William Morrow, 2011).
12   Judith Butler, "Is Kinship Already Always Heterosexual," *Differences: A Journal of Feminist Cultural Studies* 13/1 (2002): 18. Butler is talking here about debates on gay marriage, but her comments about who is or is not considered "thinkable" and "legible" extend to all kinds of non-normative lives.
13   Deepak Chopra, *The Book of Secrets* (New York: Harmony Books, 2004), 22, 103.
14   Deepak Chopra, *Ageless Body, Timeless Mind* (New York: Harmony Books, 1993), 8.
15   "Michael Jackson Was Like Krishna," excerpts from an interview on CNN Asia, transcribed in *The Times*

of India, February 25, 2012. http://timesofindia.
indiatimes.com/life-style/Michael-Jackson-was-
like-Krishna/articleshow/12018560.cms. Thanks to
Lisha McDuff for pointing me to this article and
also to "Can You Feel It."

16 Michael Jackson, *Dancing the Dream* (New York:
Doubleday, 1992), 136.

17 "Plainsong Soars Up the Charts," *The Independent*,
Tuesday,   March   29,   1994.   http://www.
independent.co.uk/news/plainsong-soars-up-the-
charts-1432273.html

18 David Metzer, "The Power Ballad," *Popular Music*
31/3 (2012): 448. The housewives quote is from
David Fricke, "Heavy Metal Justice," *Rolling Stone*,
January 12, 1989.

19 Metzer, "Power Ballad," 438.

20 Metzer, "Power Ballad," 446.

21 Vogel, *Man in the Music*, 163.

22 A point also made by Vogel, *Man in the Music*,
164–5.

23 Harvey Sachs, *The Ninth: Beethoven and the World in
1824* (New York: Random House, 2011), 1.

24 Sachs, *The Ninth*, 2.

25 Michael Dyson, "Michael Jackson's Postmodern
Spirituality," *Reflecting Black: African-American
Cultural Criticism* (Minneapolis: University of
Minnesota Press, 1993), 38.

26 Dyson, 41.

27 Mikal Gilmore, "Triumph and Tragedy," *Michael
by the Editors of Rolling Stone* (New York: Harper,
2009), 14.

Coda

1   Tim Riley, *Tell Me Why: A Beatles Commentary* (New York: Knopf, 1988), 225.

2   See Willa Stillwater's discussion in *M Poetica: Michael Jackson's Art of Connection and Defiance* (Kindle Edition, 2011).

3   Armond White, *Keep Moving: The Michael Jackson Chronicles* (New York: Resistance Works, 2009), 2–4.

Also available in the series